DRIVE AROUND
DENMARK

A handy guide for the motorist

ROBERT SPARK

GW00371204

TRAFTON PUBLISHING

Companion volumes:
DRIVE AROUND SWEDEN
DRIVE AROUND NORWAY

First published 1984.
Second edition 1986.
Third edition 1989.
Fourth edition 1993
Copyright © Trafton Publishing,
Evelyn Way, Cobham, Surrey KT11 2SJ
Text and maps © Robert Spark
ISBN 0 947890 06 8

Photographs: Pages 33, 36, 37 (upper), 38 (lower), 40, 74
(lower), 75 (upper), 76, 78 – Danish Tourist Board; pages
34, 35 (upper), 37 (lower), 38 (upper), 39 (upper), 73, 75
(lower), 77, 79, 80 – author.
Cover: The gatehouse of Valdemars Castle on the lovely
island of Tåsinge (photograph: Robert Spark).

Cover design: Light Brigade Text Limited, Chertsey,
Surrey.
Maps: Stephen G. Spark.
Typesetting: Goodfellow & Egan Phototypesetting
Limited, Cambridge.
Printed in Great Britain by The Burlington Press, Foxton,
Cambridge.

CONTENTS

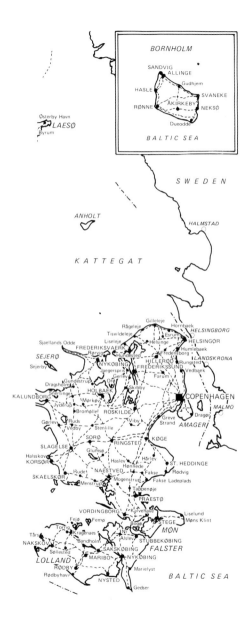

BORNHOLM

SANDVIG
ALLINGE
HASLE
Gudhjem
SVANEKE
RØNNE
AKIRKEBY
NEKSØ
Dueodde

BALTIC SEA

Østerby Havn
LAESØ
Byrum

SWEDEN

ANHOLT
HALMSTAD

KATTEGAT

Rågeleje
Gilleleje
Hornbaek
HELSINGBORG
Tisvildeleje
Esrum
Liseleje
Helsinge
HELSINGØR
Sjaellands Odde
FREDERIKSVAERK
Humlebaek
Fredensborg
Rørvig
Hundested
Rungsted
LANDSKRONA
SEJERØ
NYKØBING
HILLERØD
FREDERIKSSUND
Vedbaek
Sejerby
Jaegerspris
Gerlev
Farum
Dragsholm
Orø
Skibby
Gundestrup
HOLBAEK
KALUNDBORG
Skjertinge
Markøv
Skibby
COPENHAGEN
Jyderup
Bromølle
ROSKILDE
MALMO
Gørlev
Ruds
Greve
Vedby
Stenlille
Viby
Strand
Dragør
SORØ
AMAGER
SLAGELSE
RINGSTED
KØGE
Halsskov
Glumsø
KORSØR
Haslev
Hårlev
ST. HEDDINGE
Hønnede
Rude
NAESTVED
Fakse
Rødvig
SKAELSKØR
Mogenstrup
Fakse Ladeplads
Menstrup
Tappenøje
PRAESTØ
VORDINGBORG
Kalvehave
Liselund
Fejø
Femø
Bogø
Møns Klint
Tårs
Torrig
Kragenaes
STEGE
MØN
NAKSKOV
Bandholm
Alslev
STUBBEKØBING
Søllested
SAKSKØBING
FALSTER
LOLLAND
MARIBO
NYKØBING
RØDBY
Marielyst
Rødbyhavn
BALTIC SEA
NYSTED
Gedser

AN INTRODUCTION TO DENMARK

FOR A MOTORING holiday Denmark has a lot going for it. It is comparatively close to the UK, being our nearest neighbour across the North Sea, and can easily be reached direct by ferry or via other continental countries.

It is an enjoyable motoring country, making it especially suitable for those with little or no experience of driving abroad. There is a wide range of accommodation, food is appealing and appetising and there are plenty of things to see and do. It is a compact country which makes everywhere remarkably accessible.

English is widely spoken, the Danes are friendly and as a country it is highly civilised. All you have to accept are the limitations of its climate and topography.

COMPACT AND VARIED

Denmark is the smallest of the Scandinavian countries with an area of 16,600 square miles (43,000 square kilometres) which makes it not much more than half the size of Scotland. It consists of the Jutland peninsula and between 400 and 500 islands, of which about 100 are inhabited. The map in this introduction will show you how the parts of Denmark fit together.

There is a widely held belief that Denmark is flat and therefore scenically boring. This is a misconception. There may be no mountains (the highest point is less than 600ft above sea level), no dramatic scenery, no wide surging rivers, but instead you have an ever-changing panorama: undulating countryside, lakes, small streams and placid rivers, forests and gentle fjords. There are many areas of considerable beauty while even the 'average' landscape is very easy on the eye, incredibly neat and tidy and well groomed.

With 4,500 miles of coastline you are never more than 33 miles from the sea and there is an abundance of good beaches with long stretches of sand (on the Jutland coast you can even drive from one town to another along the beach).

Around five million inhabitants provide a fairly high population density but this is not apparent, as four fifths of all Danes are town dwellers. In fact a quarter of the inhabitants live in greater Copenhagen. Away from the larger centres of population you will find quiet towns and villages and on the minor roads you have the feeling of being very much away from it all.

Agriculture is nowhere near as important to Denmark as it was, say 25 years ago, and this has inevitably changed the appearance of the countryside. There are fewer cows in the meadow and much bigger fields of cereal crops. Pigs, closely associated with the great British breakfast, are rarely seen out of doors but are reared under cover.

Industry has greatly expanded, but as this is a comparatively recent development, factories are modern and often located in estates on the outskirts of towns.

DESIGNED FOR TOURING

Being quite small and compact you can see a great deal of Denmark without an undue amount of driving. This mean you can afford to take it easy, and take time to pause and see places of interest along your route.

As in any European country tourism is important to Denmark but it has never been allowed to overwhelm the country. You will find no major resorts, or serried ranks of high rise hotels (in fact it is very much a low-rise country) and there are no developments which form a great blot on the landscape. Of course there are areas which attract more holiday makers, but overall you are visiting a working country not a glorified theme park.

Roads are good, including the minor ones, while the islands add to your pleasure, whether you reach them by bridge or ferry.

PARTS OF DENMARK

The peninsula of Jutland (the Danes call it *Jylland*) stretches for 250 miles from the German border in the south to the northern tip where the Skagerrak meets the Kattegat. On the west coast is

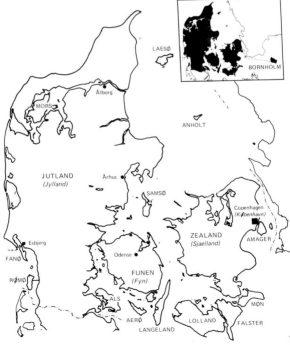

AN INTRODUCTION TO DENMARK

Esbjerg, the main port of entry for British visitors. The Jutland scenery varies from the flat marshlands of the south-west to the beautiful lake district in the centre of the peninsula and from large areas of heathland to extensive forests. On the eastern coast is the charming Djursland peninsula while the west coast offers mile after mile of firm sandy beaches, often backed by sandhills. There are two major cities: Århus and Ålborg, both with their own appeal and personality.

Funen (or *Fyn* to the Danes), linked to Jutland by two bridges, is often – and deservedly – called Denmark's garden isle. Picturesque thatched cottages and quiet moated manor houses and castles help to make this one of the most delightful parts of Denmark. The principal town is Odense, almost in the centre of the island, and the birthplace of Hans Christian Andersen.

Funen's main off-shore islands of Ærø, Tåsinge and Langeland are also most attractive: Ærø, an absolute gem, is reached by ferry, but the other two are connected by bridges.

Moving further east is Zealand (*Sjælland*) which is separated from Funen by the 18-mile wide Great Belt. Large ferries maintain a constant service across this busy stretch of water although it is now being bridged and very soon you will drive across. Zealand also has its quota of beaches, forests, lakes and farmland but it is dominated on the eastern side by Copenhagen. 'Wonderful Copenhagen' is not just an empty phrase, it really is a most enjoyable city: friendly, with a compact centre, offering a wide range of attractions. Less than 30 miles away is Helsingør (often known to us as Elsinore) which is dominated by Kronborg Castle, famous as the setting for Shakespeare's 'Hamlet'.

To the south of Zealand are the islands of Lolland, Falster and Møn. You cannot get away from the fact that Lolland is flat, but it has some good beaches while Falster is similarly endowed but is a little more undulating. Møn, smallest island of the three, is different again having steep chalk cliffs on its eastern side. All three are linked by bridges, have some nice little towns and a lot of tranquil countryside.

Eighty-five miles away from the rest of Denmark is the Baltic island of Bornholm. This beautiful holiday island, with an area of 225 square miles has an attractive mix of rich farmland, white beaches, a rocky coastline and one of Denmark's largest forests. It is reached by ferry from Copenhagen and is well worth a visit.

A PLACE TO STAY

Denmark offers a wide range of accommodation: luxury hotels, inns, youth hostels, camping sites, summerhouses, farmhouses and apartments in town and country. Summerhouses are particularly popular, as are the holiday hotels. The latter are self-catering centres with apartments or flats and a central building providing a range of amenities.

FOOD AND DRINK

There is a separate chapter on this subject but to put it briefly: Danish food is appetising and enjoyable. There is considerable emphasis on fish and seafood (and very good it is) while typical Danish dishes feature quite widely as well as the usual 'international' fare. The famous help yourself 'Cold Table' (*Koldt Bord*) is not seen as much as it used to be, but I am pleased to report that the equally well known open sandwiches (*Smørrebrød*) are flourishing in all their numerous varieties.

Domestically produced alcoholic beverages mean beer – who doesn't know the famous names of Carlsberg and Tuborg – and aquavit (schnapps). Apart from one or two liqueurs, and something to keep the cold out or settle a hangover called Gammel Dansk, that is it. Wines and spirits are imported and while the former are fairly reasonable (and often bottled in Denmark) the latter are distinctly expensive.

TIDY AND TOLERANT

Denmark is clean and neat (but not without its quota of graffiti) with high standards of hygiene. The Danes tend to be an even-tempered and tolerant nation – sometimes described as a little boring which is no bad thing in this rather turbulent world. This doesn't mean that the inhabitants never complain about their Government, income tax or some other imposition, while they have even rebelled against the EC.

The country has a high standard of living, an advanced social welfare system and the population is increasingly concerned about the environment. Denmark is the oldest constitutional monarchy in Europe, a parliamentary democracy and the only Scandinavian country in the European Community (although that is likely to change soon when Sweden becomes a member).

WEATHER

Just as the topography of Denmark is often misunderstood by the British so is the Danish climate. It is a temperate climate with rather mild winters when compared with the rest of Scandinavia and variable summers (just like the UK). Summer temperatures average 18 – 25 deg C (64 – 77 deg F) but the weather is changeable and it changes quickly from sunshine to showers and back again. It is seldom completely calm and, in particular, the west side of Jutland has a reputation for being windy – which can be very exhilarating. Spring and autumn are often very enjoyable.

THINGS TO SEE AND DO

There is no shortage of things to see and do – ranging from fascinating remains of the Viking age to superb modern art galleries. There are many intriguing museums – particularly the open air ones – and plenty of opportunities for sports and pastimes: golf, fishing, swimming, sailing, riding, walking and cycling. At many places (and at an increasing number of hotels) you can hire a bicycle. There are well-surfaced cycle tracks and these are increasing all the time. Whereas in the past Danes cycled because it was their established mode of transport, now they do it more for recreation and the sake of their health. Incidentally, much of what is in this guide is just as valid for someone wanting a cycling holiday as for the motorist.

There are plenty of activities for children who are positively liked as opposed to being tolerated. After all, this is a country which has produced both Hans Christian Andersen *and* Lego.

DRIVE AROUND DENMARK

This is the fourth completely updated edition of Drive around Denmark and its aim and purpose remain unchanged: a compact guide which is informative, practical and designed to lead you to some of the most attractive areas in this small and inviting country. Use it to take you off the main roads and down some of the charming minor byways and to smaller and lesser known places.

I hope you will share my enjoyment of this delightful country and having made one visit that you will want to return again and again. The friendliness and warmth of the Danes more than makes up for any lack of mountains, guaranteed sunshine or cheap wine.

My thanks to the Danish Tourist Board, including the UK Director and in particular Britt Sander, for their ever ready assistance. I would also like to thank the UK management of Scandinavian Seaways for their co-operation. Finally to all those Danes who offered help and information – even though many of them were unconnected with tourism – thank you very much.

GETTING THERE

PASSENGER ships have been sailing regularly between Britain and Denmark for over 125 years. The company that started this link across the North Sea – DFDS – is the same one that maintains the service today, although it now sails under the name of Scandinavian Seaways. I have been sailing this direct route to Denmark for well over 30 years and during that time there have been many changes, the most notable one being that the ships are far larger today.

Going by sea has some less obvious advantages. For example, however much you have had to panic to get away, once you are on board you can relax for about the next 19 hours. The facilities on board now allow you to have a short cruise before your holiday – and another one at the end of it.

Scandinavian Seaways operate a year round service from Harwich and a summer only service from Newcastle, both to the west Jutland port of Esbjerg. In 1993 the Harwich service was up to four times weekly and the Newcastle service twice a week (April–September). Both services are subject to change each year.

On the Harwich-Esbjerg route are the *Dana Anglia* (14,400 tons), and either the *Prince of Scandinavia* or *Princess of Scandinavia* (15,795 tons). These ships are a far cry from the ferries of the past and are much more closely related to small cruise liners. All three are air-conditioned and stabilised and have had considerable sums of money spent on them in recent years. The AA gave all three ships a 5-star rating in 1992.

The Newcastle-Esbjerg service is currently served by the smaller *Winston Churchill* (8,657 tons) whose classic lines have given it an enthusiastic following. How much longer it will remain in service is debatable.

The bigger ships on the Harwich route have a wider range of amenities on board; a choice of restaurants, a lounge with entertainment in the evening (which can be variable in quality), several cinemas, a disco, a pub and bars, shops, children's play area and cabins with private shower and toilet.

If you want to pamper yourself you can always opt for *Commodore Class* which provides a de-luxe cabin, spacious and well-equipped, and even breakfast in bed if you want it.

For the family traveller with children the best choice for a meal is the help-yourself Scandinavian Buffet where for a fixed price you can eat as much as you like (there are reduced prices for children). The fast food cafe is useful and the help-yourself breakfast buffet is also good value.

Children also have their own Pirates Club with films, entertainment and competitions and this keeps them occupied for part of the voyage.

The facilities on the *Winston Churchill* are not quite up to the same standard and only some of the cabins have private

11

shower and toilet. This ship received a 3-star rating from the AA.

If you like a pre-dinner drink when you are on holiday it is advisable to buy your supplies on board ship rather than pay the high prices in Denmark. But don't expect any substantial bargains in the on-board shops.

Payment for meals, drinks and shop purchases can be in sterling or Danish kroner and any of the usual credit cards are accepted.

Of course the North Sea is not always placid but the size of the ships plus their stabilisers help to reduce the motion and if that is not enough, the information office on board has available some effective pills. So don't be put off by tales about the North Sea.

What is common to all Scandinavian Seaways ships is a high standard of cleanliness and well-turned out crews.

VIA GERMANY

Should you find that you cannot get a booking on the Esbjerg route, don't worry, there is an alternative which is the Scandinavian Seaways service to Hamburg. There are departures every other day all year round from Harwich while there is a twice weekly service from Newcastle (April–September).

A glance at the map will show that from Hamburg it's an easy drive to south Jutland. If you are heading for Copenhagen you can take the one hour ferry crossing from Puttgarden to Rødby on the island of Lolland and then drive on the E47.

OTHER ALTERNATIVES

Other alternatives are to use Stena Sealink's service from Harwich to the Hook of Holland or Dover to Calais and then use the excellent motorway network on the Continent. Then there is Olau Line's route from Sheerness to Vlissingen in Holland. They have day and night sailings, and their two mega-ferries are very well appointed and have AA 5-star ratings.

Finally you can fly to Århus, Billund or Copenhagen and rent a car – it saves time but is less convenient. The advantage of taking your own car is that you can put everything in the boot.

PACKAGING YOUR HOLIDAY

If the idea of going to Denmark independently is too daunting on your first visit there are packages which still let you have the freedom to go-as-you-please. For example Scandinavian Seaways offer arrangements featuring hotels, inns, youth and family hostels and camping. They also have all kinds of self-catering arrangements if you prefer to stay in one place and just make day excursions in the surrounding district.

There are several other operators who also offer variations

on the go-as-you-please theme or who will tailor make arrangements for you. They include Scantours, Specialised Tours and Sovereign Scanscape.

REMINDERS

The Harwich-Esbjerg service departs from Parkeston Quay where there have been improvements to the terminal. The approach is well-signed and the road from the A12 has also improved over the last few years. The check-in time is 90 minutes before sailing.

The terminal for the Newcastle service is at North Shields. You take the A817 (Howdon Road) near the northern entrance to the Tyne Tunnel and look for the signed right-turn to Tyne Commission Quay.

At Esbjerg the ships berth at Englandskajen and on leaving the port area the roads are clearly signed whichever direction you are going. If you are heading east on the E20 (the main road across Jutland from Esbjerg) you are routed around the town, avoiding the centre. Coming in to Esbjerg on the E20 the signs are equally clear. Access to the car deck is not always permitted during the voyage so when you leave your car take what you need during the crossing but avoid having to heave heavy baggage to and fro (there are lifts, but a small overnight bag is much more satisfactory) Do not forget to lock your car (doors and boot) and switch off lights if they happen to be on.

If you leave the UK on a Friday or a Saturday remember that when you arrive in Denmark the banks (and shops) will be closed. Also the Danes have a number of public holidays that can catch you out – for example would you know when Great Prayer Day is celebrated? (For the answer turn to page 141).

DRIVING IN DENMARK

FOR THE BRITISH MOTORIST, Denmark must rate as one of the easiest European countries in which to drive. In fact, I would go further and say it is *the* easiest, because of its excellent road network, lack of natural hazards and the generally acceptable level of competence and discipline of Danish road users. In addition the road signing tends to be good and towns are usually provided with adequate parking facilities.

All these features make it an ideal destination for the first time abroad motorist and should encourage those who may have qualms about venturing overseas with their car.

The disadvantages really reduce themselves to two: driving on the right and the Danish language. Driving on the right is common to all European countries, other than Britain and Ireland, and really presents no problems. Once you have been driving for a very short time it becomes quite natural. Care needs to be taken when starting off after a break or first thing in the morning or when you are on deserted roads. You also need to 'think right' at roundabouts and when turning. Overtaking also requires more care and a reliable front seat passenger can be a help – but the accent must be on reliable.

The language is not such a problem: the standard international road signs are used in Denmark and there are not that many domestic ones you need worry about (some of them are mentioned later in this chapter). As so many Danes speak English there is far less likelihood of difficulty if you have a problem with your car, or get lost or if you have an emergency of some kind.

One thing which you should have with you – particularly if you are going to make the best use of this book and get the most out of your holiday – are good maps. I cannot stress too highly the value of good maps as they do let you get so much more out of a visit to Denmark, apart from avoiding that 'I wonder where we are now' kind of feeling. I recommend the Færdselskort 1:200,000 which are published in four parts by the Danish Geodætisk Institut. Map 1 covers northern Jutland; Map 2 takes in central Jutland (from just a little north of Esbjerg) and the island of Samsø; Map 3 includes southern Jutland, Funen and the smaller islands of Tåsinge, Ærø and Langeland; and Map 4 covers Zealand and the islands of Lolland, Falster, Møn and Bornholm. You can get them at most major bookshops in Denmark and there are several map specialists that stock them in Britain, for example Stanfords Ltd., 12 Long Acre, London WC2 9LP. I always take them with me in the car and a useful feature is that the key to the various symbols and signs and so on is given in English as well as Danish.

The Danish Tourist Board's map with sights and attractions is a useful initial planner, although the scale of the maps is not really large enough if you are getting off the beaten track. Price £2.50 from the Danish Tourist Board's London office (see page 142).

THE ROAD SYSTEM

As already mentioned, Danish roads are good and present no problems. Minor roads carry relatively little traffic but the trunk routes and cross-country routes can be busy – particularly in summer. Also you have a considerable volume of commuter traffic, morning and evening around major towns and cities – especially Copenhagen. But in general motoring in Denmark is still a pleasure.

Danish roads have three number classifications: E or European routes, primary roads and secondary roads. Where I have quoted road numbers in the itineraries later in this book they are, to the best of my knowledge, identified on road signs.

Motorway construction started late in Denmark and even today the motorway routes remain incomplete. The motorways have the international 'E' description and are as follows: E20 Esbjerg-Copenhagen; E45 Padborg (German frontier) – Frederikshavn; E47 Rødbyhavn (ferry port for connection to Puttgarden in Germany) – Copenhagen – Helsingør; E55 Gedser (ferry connections to the German ports of Warnemünde and Rostock) – Copenhagen – Helsingør; E39 Ålborg – Hirtshals; E133 Snoghøj – Vejle. Esbjerg, Helsingør, Frederikshavn, Hirtshals, Rødbyhavn and Puttgarden are all ferry ports with services to other countries.

The E20 from Esbjerg to Copenhagen lacks motorway status for the first part of its route across Jutland. This is now being remedied and work should be completed by 1995.

If the motorway building programme has been sluggish then bridge building has been flourishing. Over the last 25 years numerous new bridges have been built to replace ferry connections. There are now over 25 major bridges spanning sounds, belts and fjords and all of them, like the roads and the Limfjord tunnel at Ålborg, are toll free. However that will not be the case when the new bridges across the Great Belt are completed (see internal ferries chapter).

What the Danes have achieved to a very great extent is the construction of bypasses around towns, and even villages. This has effectively removed heavy traffic from town centres, making life much more pleasant for the inhabitants. This means that you frequently have to leave the main road to get into a town. You need to watch out for direction signs; watch for those marked *Centrum*.

Not only are bypasses popular but so are pedestrian streets. Here again, even quite modest towns have pedestrianised the main shopping streets. An alternative to creating a complete pedestrian precinct has been to allow traffic, but to provide a number of artificially created obstacles to slow it down. These cause traffic to reduce speed by having to zig-zag down the street,

15

although sometimes these obstacles are regarded as merely something of a challenge to younger drivers. In general the pedestrian precincts have been dealt with in an imaginative manner and add much to the attractiveness of the town centres. Their introduction has often been linked to the restoration of buildings so that an appealing townscape has been created.

Before leaving the subject of roads it is worth mentioning that when the Danes decide to carry out major road-works it will often result in the complete closure of the thoroughfare. Traffic is diverted, sometimes over quite a distance, and in this case the sign to watch for is *Omkørsel* (diversion). Road-works are indicated by the word *Vejarbejde*, while road closed is *Vejen en spærret* and no through road is *Gennemkørsel forbudt*.

The Danish Road Directorate annually publishes a very useful little English-language brochure which highlights any road repairs or reconstruction taking place during the summer. Maps pin-point the position and duration of the road works. There are also details of events which might cause traffic disruption.

The booklet also contains other useful information and you can usually get a free copy at local tourist offices. It's extremely useful – especially if you have a ship to catch.

RULES AND REGULATIONS

In Denmark there are three basic speed limits: in built-up areas 50 km/h (31 mph), outside built-up areas 80 km/h (50 mph) and on motorways 100 km/h (62 mph). When towing a caravan or trailer the speed limit is 70 km/h (44 mph). Local signs may show lower or higher limits and the general rule is that you should adjust your speed to the prevailing circumstances.

There is no specific sign showing the permitted speed when you approach a built-up area (as with the '30' sign in the UK). Instead you take your cue from the town name sign which also includes a silhouette of buildings: that is where the 50 km/h limit begins. When you leave the town you will find the sign repeated, this time with a diagonal red line through it, ending the speed restriction. In the case of a speed limit offence you are liable to a heavy fine which has to be paid on the spot. If you cannot pay, your car may be detained – and the police do not accept credit cards.

As already mentioned, the basic rule is drive on the right and overtake on the left. You should give way to traffic from the right. In particular watch for the triangular red and white give way signs or the line of white triangles painted across the road (known locally as shark's teeth) which indicate that you must give way to traffic on the road you are entering. You must also give way to buses when they signal that they are pulling out from a bus stop and, of course, avoid travelling in a designated bus lane. Denmark has no trams, so that is one less hazard to worry about.

DRIVING IN DENMARK

What is particularly important is that at junctions or round-abouts you must give way to pedestrians crossing the road you are entering. When turning left you move across in front of the traffic coming from the opposite direction and turning left, not behind as in the UK. Major junctions often have painted 'turn marks' on the roads to guide you to your correct position. Traffic lights are similar to the UK but they are sometimes suspended from above the centre of the road. In some instances filter lights are incorporated.

Another important point when making a right turn is to watch for cyclists and mopeds. They usually have their own marked or separate track on the right hand side of the road and if they are going straight ahead you must give way to them. Where the bicycle/moped lane is only marked by a white line (and not a separate track) you should not cross it. In fact the golden rule is to keep a sharp eye open for cyclists – they have their rights as well as motorists.

Clear indications should be given when you are turning and, in particular, when you may be changing lanes on motorways or main roads. Copenhagen, like any capital city, requires more care and attention. On the whole, Danish drivers are considerate towards those with a foreign registration.

Your horn should only be used in case of danger, instead you can flash your headlamps as a warning. Dipped headlights must always be used throughout the 24 hours, parking lights are not sufficient. Using only one headlight or spotlight is not allowed. Motorcyclists must use dipped headlamps, even by day and in clear weather.

The regulations say that cars with asymmetric headlights for left hand driving may only be used if the part of the lens from which the asymmetric beam issues is covered with some opaque material. The material – I always use black plastic insulating tape – is cut to cover the appropriate area and applied to the outer surface of the headlight. You can also buy kits for different makes of cars with the black self-adhesive material marked out to the right shape.

Perhaps one of the most important laws that affects visiting motorists to Denmark is that relating to drinking and driving. All the Scandinavian countries are tough on drink/drive offenders. You can be prosecuted for having either an excess of alcohol in the blood or for driving with an undue proportion of alcohol in the blood. And just to show the law is even handed on the subject you can even be prosecuted for the same offence if you are riding a horse. Prosecution for an excess of alcohol carries an almost certain sentence of detention or imprisonment. You are liable to prosecution if the quantity of alcohol in the blood exceeds 0.8 per cent. Moral: don't drink and drive.

The driver and all passengers must wear seat belts if your car is fitted with them. A motor-cyclist must wear a crash helmet and this also applies, of course, to a pillion passenger. Carrying a warning triangle is another requirement.

When taking your car to Denmark you will need your valid driving licence (not a provisional one), the certificate of registration, and your car should have a GB plate or sticker. (If you are travelling with Scandinavian Seaways or taking one of their packages you will normally get a sticker with your tickets.)

An insurance 'green card' is no longer essential for a vehicle registered in Britain but having one is strongly recommended. Consult your insurance company on this point. It is also worth checking whether you are covered for damage in transit.

PARKING

An important aspect of motoring is parking. Fortunately in Denmark parking is not too great a problem. The Danes have quite sensibly realised that if a lot of people have cars they need somewhere to park them. For example, in towns where there are pedestrian streets there are invariably parking areas nearby and you just need to look for the 'P' signs as you near the town centre. Although there may be a limit on how long you can park, at least you will not have to pay (except in major cities).

These are the parking regulation signs you will see:

Parkering/Standsning Forbudt. No parking or stopping.

Under three minutes stopping or stopping for passengers, or loading, is not regarded as parking.

Datostop/Datoparkering. Stopping or parking allowed on even dates on the side of the street with even numbered premises and on odd dates on the side with odd numbers.

Where limited waiting is permitted the times will be shown on the signs – hours shown in black are for Monday to Friday; in black and in brackets are for Saturday; and hours shown in red are for Sunday. Very often they only show Monday – Friday and Saturday times. Parking discs (*P-Skive*) are required whenever waiting is limited. You can get one, free of charge, from petrol stations, post offices, police stations, most tourist offices and some banks. When you park you set the hand on the disc to point to the quarter hour following the time of arrival. The disc is then placed – facing outwards – against the inside of the windscreen on the side nearest the curb.

Parking is forbidden on or in front of pedestrian crossings, within 5 metres (16½ft) of a road junction, on cycle tracks, in front of fire hydrants, where the kerb near a bus stop is painted yellow or otherwise within 12 metres (39ft) of a bus stop sign. You may park with two wheels on the pavement providing you don't inconvenience pedestrians and local police regulations allow it. (In Copenhagen parking on pavements is only allowed in marked areas.) Parking is not permitted in play streets.

In major cities with parking meters these are in operation from 9.00am to 6.00pm Mondays to Fridays and 9.00am to 1.00pm Saturdays. The maximum period is three hours and they accept one krone, five kroner or 10 kroner coins. In Copenhagen they have different charges, depending on the location of the meter (details later in this chapter).

If you park illegally you can get a written ticket placed on your car or you can be towed away which means you have to pay the tow charge, a garage fee and possibly a fine.

THE FUEL SUPPLY

Petrol stations are reasonably plentiful throughout the country and all the usual international brands are available. The vast majority are self-service (*selvbetjening* or *tank selv*). Many stations now have note acceptors which let you get petrol after hours. They take Dkr 50 or Dkr 100 notes and those I have seen have pictorial instructions which make them fairly easy to follow. Petrol is usually available in a choice of three octane ratings but small rural outlets may only offer one rating. Lead-free petrol is widely available and the pump is identified by the word '*Blyfri*'. One pump may well be for diesel so don't go putting the wrong fuel in your tank. Petrol is, of course, sold by the litre.

BREAKDOWNS AND ACCIDENTS

If you have a breakdown look in the telephone directory under *Automobil reparation* or call *Falck*. This is a national organisation which has fire engines, ambulances and salvage equipment. You can call Falck day or night and they will come out and if they can't solve the problem on the spot they will tow you to the nearest garage. They charge a fee for this service. Falck have over 100 centres all over the country.

On motorways you can use the emergency telephones and call Falck.

At major garages you are likely to find someone who speaks English and all leading manufacturers have service workshops in Denmark. Don't forget that value added tax at the rate of 25 per cent - labour and materials – is added to all repair bills.

Should you have the misfortune to be involved in an accident you should get in touch with the *Dansk Forening for International Motorkøretøjsforsikring*, Amaliegade 10, DK-1256 Copenhagen K - telephone 33 13 75 55. Following an accident you should leave the car where it is and make sure all essential particulars are noted. It is suggested that if the vehicle is causing a serious obstruction you should mark its position before independent witnesses and if possible take a photograph of the scene. This seems to be asking a lot of someone just involved in an accident. If you want emergency services dial 112 (no coins needed in call boxes). Finally, don't forget to notify your own insurance company as quickly as possible.

The national motoring organisation in Denmark is the *FDM – Forenede Danske Motorejere*. They offer technical and legal assistance, together with general tourist information, to members of motoring organisations affiliated to the AIT. They don't have a breakdown service but they have offices in about 40 towns. Their head office address and telephone number is Firskovvej 32, P.O. Box 500, DK-2800 Lyngby, Telephone 45 93 08 00, Fax 45 93 32 42.

PARKING IN COPENHAGEN

For parking purposes central Copenhagen is divided into red, yellow, green or blue zones. There are both parking meters and pay and display arrangements (you get your ticket from a kerbside parkomat machine and you display it on the inside of the windscreen on the left-hand side). Parking fees are payable between 8.00am and 6.00pm on weekdays in all zones and also between 8.00am and 2.00pm on Saturdays and Sundays in yellow and blue zones. Current charges are as follows:

Red zone Dkr 15 per hour max stay 3 hours.
Yellow zone Dkr 9 per hour max stay 10 hours
Green zone Dkr 6 per hour max stay 10 hours
Blue zone Dkr 4 per hour max stay 10 hours
There is some kerbside parking using a parking disc and where you can park for up to one hour free of charge.

Multi-storey car parks usually open 6.00a.m. or 8.00a.m. to 8.00p.m. or midnight. Some close on Saturday afternoons or Sundays. Average rates: 2 hours Dkr 10.- to 15.- rising to Dkr 30.- to 40,- per day.

ROAD SIGNS – SOME EXAMPLES

No entry	*Inkørsel forbudt*
Diversion	*Omkørsel*
Cul-de-Sac	*Blind vej*
Road closed	*Vejen en spærret*
No through road	*Gennemkørsel forbudt*
One way street	*Ensrettet*
Exit	*Udkørsel*
Soft shoulders	*Rabatten er blød*
Road works	*Vejarbejde*
Danger	*Fare*
Right	*Højre*
Left	*Venstre*
Pedestrians	*Fodgængere*
Cycle track	*Cykelsti*

INTERNAL FERRIES

A QUICK glance at the map of Denmark is sufficient to tell you that ferries are an essential means of communication. Although many bridges have been built – and some are outstanding examples of the bridge builders' skill – there are still 47 internal ferry routes in Denmark, plus another 32 serving other countries. Car ferries are, in fact, a way of life, a basic requirement and, large or small, they operate with a humdrum efficiency which would put many other forms of transport to shame.

Crossing times vary from two minutes to seven hours and the sizes of the ferries range from workaday little vessels with space for a handful of cars to massive multi-deck examples which take over 400 cars at a time. Making a ferry crossing is a pleasant interlude in the day's driving and some routes provide a most enjoyable mini-cruise. Any route that takes around 20 minutes or more will have some sort of refreshment facilities on board, while the vessels on the longer journeys may have both a cafeteria and a restaurant, a kiosk, comfortable seating and even a children's play area.

The Danes make the most of their ferries – coming on board and sunning themselves on deck, consuming picnics, or having refreshments, reading, chatting or dozing. In other words, making the most of the break from driving.

On the longer routes you can reserve your car space and in summer this is certainly advisable. On several of the most important connections I would regard it as essential. On any of the services operated by the Danish State Railways (DSB) – with one exception which will be mentioned later – you can make the reservation at any railway station. On other routes the reservation can be made by telephone (your hotel or the local tourist office will oblige). In each case you need to know how long in advance you need to arrive at the ferry berth. On the internal routes it is usually quite minimal, such as 15 minutes before departure.

On the short crossings there are no reservation facilities and you just turn up and take the next available departure with space. Nearly all these operate a very frequent service although there are the exceptions which run 'on demand'. How long you may have to wait on some of these short non-reservable services is very difficult to estimate. It depends on the time of the year and the day of the week and, for example, if there are trucks or buses waiting to cross at these can rapidly fill up the deck space of a small vessel. You need to allow for some delays when calculating your journey time, particularly if it is in the peak summer period or at the weekend.

The cost of the ferry should also be taken into account and these of course vary greatly depending on the length of the crossing. For a car and driver the single fare can range from Dkr 26 (for a 10 minute crossing) to Dkr 532 (for a seven hour crossing). Return fares sometimes offer a reduction and there are also some special offers: day returns, low season reductions and so on. On a few of the services to small islands, only return fares are available. There is no doubt that on one or two routes the small capacity of the ferries is one effective means of keeping the flow of visitors and their cars to reasonable proportions.

THE GREAT BELT MOTORWAY

By far the most important ferry route is that crossing the Great Belt (*Storebælt*) and linking Funen and Zealand. Large car ferries are ceaselessly ploughing across the Belt from the purpose-built terminals at Knudshoved (Funen) and Halsskov (Zealand).

By the end of the decade this will have changed completely as construction is well under way on a fixed link across the Great Belt. There will be a road and rail bridge from Funen to the tiny island of Sprogø where an immense road suspension bridge will then stretch to Zealand. The rail lines won't use this bridge but will go through a tunnel. Instead of a 50-minute ferry crossing you will be able to drive across, on average, in 11 minutes – but you will of course pay a substantial toll for the privilege.

If you want to see how this huge civil engineering project is progressing there are Great Belt exhibition centres by the ferry terminals at Halsskov on Zealand and Knudshoved on Funen. (Look for the signs '*Storebaelt Udstillingscenter*').

Once on board the ferry and parked you can make for the restaurant, cafeteria, seating area or go on deck, but do check which staircase serves your part of the car deck and on which deck you are parked. The staircases have a letter (*Trappe A, B, C* and so on) and when it comes to seeking your car among 400 others on several levels you need to know where to find it.

The crossing time is an hour and as you approach your destination there will be a loudspeaker announcement. On the car deck there are two lines of lights above each line of cars. These are red until a lane is about to move when they change to green. Don't start up before you get the green otherwise you will be very unpopular with your fellow motorists. I should add that these lights are not always used. Reservations on this route are essential, particularly if you are heading for Esbjerg and the ship for England. If you miss your booked time you may have quite a wait and they will not make an exception for those with ships to catch elsewhere. If you arrive early you will often get on an earlier sailing, which means you can take it a little more leisurely on the next section of your journey. You can buy your ticket in advance or pay at the check-in booth. Tickets and reservations can be dealt with by Scandinavian Seaways in the UK as they are the general agents for the Danish State Railways.

There are several other important routes linking Jutland and Zealand and on any of these a reservation is desirable. They include the Mols Line service from Ebeltoft to Sj. Odde (Duration 1 hour 40 minutes) which has very modern large ferries; Grenå – Hundested (duration 2 hours 40 minutes); and Århus – Kalundborg (duration 3 hours 10 minutes). The longest service is that between Copenhagen and Rønne, on the island of Bornholm (duration 7 hours) and this has large well-equipped vessels with lounges, lying down and cabin accommodation.

OTHER ROUTES

Some of the services serving the smaller islands are highly enjoyable and of them I would rate the one between Svendborg and Ærøskøbing on the island of Ærø as the best. You sail down the Svendborg Sound, between Funen and Tåsinge, past some smaller islands to the idyllic little town of Ærøskøbing. It takes 70 minutes and on a fine day it is superb. Others play an essential role in any island-hopping itinerary (and there are several of those to be found in this book).

Earlier I mentioned there was one Danish State Railways route for which advance reservations are not available. This is the 20 minute link from Esbjerg to the island of Fanø. This is the island which you see as you arrive on your ship from Britain. Although there are frequent crossings (30–34 per day) the car capacity is very limited and in the height of summer this can result in a wait of up to four hours or longer before you drive on board. So if you have a little time to spare at Esbjerg and decide to take your car to Fanø bear in mind you might have a long wait to get back. There would be nothing more annoying than to be on the island and to watch your ship to England sailing away without you. So near and yet so far!

On the shorter crossings you frequently pay on board – the ticket seller somehow getting round everyone before the ferry arrives at its destination.

The approaches to the ferries, even the smallest ones, are always clearly signed and in the same way, on leaving the ferry your route is always well signposted.

INTERNATIONAL ROUTES

The 32 international ferry routes provide connections from Denmark to Britain, Norway, Sweden, Poland, Germany and the Faroe Islands. Some of these are particularly popular with the Danes as they allow them to buy duty free goods – hence the reason that thousands of passengers cross stretches of water for no other real purpose.

INTERNAL FERRY ROUTES

The figures in brackets are the number of departures per day (in summer). This is followed by the crossing time. The figure that follows is the cost, one way, for a car and two persons (1992 fares).

INTERNAL FERRIES

1. Copenhagen – Rønne
(1–2), 7 hrs, Dkr 726
2. Ebeltoft – Sj. Odde
(6–10), 1 hr 40 mins, Dkr 300.
3. Grenå – Hundested
(3), 2 hrs 40 mins, Dkr 330
4. Århus – Kalundborg
(2–8), 3 hrs, Dkr 200
5. Kalundborg – Juelsminde
(2–5), 3 hrs, Dkr 260
6. Halsskov – Knudshoved
(19–32), 1 hr, Dkr 200–410
7. Korsør – Nyborg
(17–24), 1 hr 10 mins, Dkr 195
8. Korsør – Lohals
(2–4), 1 hr 15 mins, Dkr 220
9. Stigsnæs – Agersø
(9–14), 15 mins, Dkr 233–308 (return)
10. Stigsnæs – Omø
(5–8), 40 mins, Dkr 215–280 (return)
11. Kalundborg – Kolby Kås
(3–4), 2 hrs, Dkr 275
12. Havnsø – Sejerø
(4–5), 1 hr, Dkr 230 (return)
13. Holbæk – Orø
(7–10), 30 mins, Dkr 58
14. Hammer Bakke – Orø
(on request), 6 mins, Dkr 88 (return)
15. Kulhuse – Sølager
(on request), 8 mins, Dkr 44
16. Hundested – Rørvig
(10–13), 25 mins, Dkr 110
17. Tårs – Spodsbjerg
(16–20), 45 mins, Dkr 215
18. Kragenæs – Fejø
(16–21), 15 mins, Dkr 72 (return)
19. Kragenæs – Femø
(6–8), 50 mins, Dkr 139 (return)
20. Bandholm – Askø
(5–8), 30 mins, Dkr 129 (return)
21. Stubbekøbing – Bogø
(8–20), 12 mins, Dkr 50
22. Bøjden – Fynshav
(7–8), 50 mins, Dkr 146
23. Fåborg – Avernakø – Lyø
(5–8), 40–60 mins, Dkr 110
24. Svendborg – Skarø – Drejø
(2–4), 50–90 mins, Dkr 85

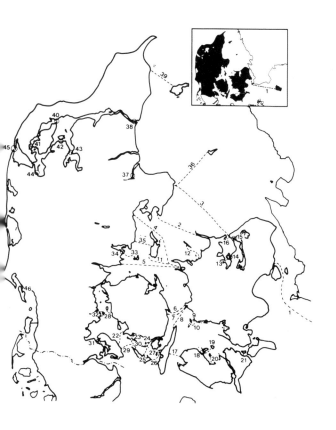

25. Svendborg – Ærøskøbing
(4–5), 1 hr 10 mins, Dkr 151
26. Rudkøbing – Marstal
(4–5), 1 hr, Dkr 151
27. Rudkøbing – Strynø
(4–9), 35 mins, Dkr 120 (return)
28. Assens – Bågø
(4–6), 30 mins, Dkr 150 (return)
29. Mommark – Søby
(2–5), 1 hr 5 mins, Dkr 151
30. Fåborg – Søby
(4–6), 1 hr, Dkr 151

INTERNAL FERRIES

31. Ballebro – Hardeshøj
(29–33), 10 mins, Dkr 30–36
32. Årøsund – Årø
(14–16), 10 mins, Dkr 56 (return)
33. Snaptun – Endelave
(1–4), 1 hr 10 mins, Dkr 250 (return)
34. Snaptun – Hjarnø
(25), 5 mins, Dkr 57 (return)
35. Hov – Sælvig
(5–9), 1 hr 20 mins, Dkr 189
36. Grenå – Anholt
(1–2), 2 hrs 45 mins, Dkr 460–610
37. Udbyhøj Nord – Udbyhøj Sud
(on request), 5 mins, Dkr 32
38. Hals – Egense
(40–60), 5 mins, Dkr 31
39. Frederikshavn – Læsø
(3–4), 1 hr 30 mins, Dkr 275
40. Mors – Thy (Feggesund)
(8–24), 5 mins, Dkr 35
41. Mors – Thy (Næssund)
(28–30), 5 mins, Dkr 35
42. Branden – Fur
(41–46), 5 mins, Dkr 60 (return)
43. Hvalpsund – Sundsøre
(28–29), 10 mins, Dkr 40–52
44. Kleppen – Venø
(26–40), 2 mins, Dkr 48 (return)
45. Thyborøn – Agger
(15–19), 10 mins, Dkr 42
46. Esbjerg – Fanø
(17–38), 20 mins, Dkr 245–695 (return)
(In some cases the car rate may vary and these fares should only
be regarded as guide prices.)

ACCOMMODATION – HOTELS, INNS, SELF-CATERING, CAMPING

THERE IS a wide variety of accommodation available in Denmark and the choice extends all the way from luxury hotels of the best international standard to camping sites. The motorist, being mobile, can of course select where to stay from the full range of accommodation, according to personal preference.

Apart from hotels in various price categories, there are inns (in Danish *kro*) many of which are very picturesque and old-established, and these are to be found in the country, in villages or small towns. There are the holiday hotels and holiday centres – self-catering establishments, invariably by the sea, which are now very popular and farmhouse holidays. Another Danish phenomenon is the summerhouse which are to be found all over the country and provide another category of self-catering accommodation.

Youth and family hostels are available for those on a budget and they are open to motorists (of any age) while there are hundreds of camping sites to choose from if you want to keep expenditure to a minimum.

Over 1,000 establishments are listed in the Danish Tourist Board's brochure on hotels, pensions, inns, motels and holiday centres. A copy is available, free of charge, from the DTB's London office and it is a very useful publication to have with you. There is no system of grading or stars for hotels, etc., so you have to be guided by price. Unfortunately a growing number of establishments do not include prices in the DTB's guide which is an annoying trend. Prices quoted (in the brochure or when you receive information direct from the hotel, etc.) will include service and VAT (known as *Moms*).

Accommodation in Copenhagen can be arranged through Hotelbooking København, Bernstorffsgade 1, DK–1577 Copenhagen V. Tel: 33 12 28 80, Fax: 33 129723. You can call personally at the same address and from April 22 to September 19 they are open from 9am to midnight (shorter hours out of the main season). A booking fee is charged.

You can also use Easy-Book, Århusgade 33–35, DK–2100 Copenhagen Ø. Tel: 31 38 00 37, Fax: 31 380637. Their telephones are manned from 9am to 11pm all year round. Their service covers the whole of Denmark.

Outside Copenhagen the local tourist office will assist you with the reservation of accommodation. A small fee will be charged.

The principal hotels in cities, towns, in the country or at the seaside universally offer a high standard of accommodation. Bedrooms will invariably have a telephone and radio and often a TV, and sometimes a mini-bar, plus a well-equipped bathroom. Amenities will include a restaurant, bar and lift and, increasingly, a swimming pool, sauna and exercise room.

A number of new hotels have been built over the last two

decades and these supplement the older-established premises usually to be found in the centre of towns. Some of the latter may be rather old fashioned in their decor but they are invariably clean and comfortable. Further down the scale are pensions which provide another grade of accommodation, while many tourist offices can arrange an inexpensive stay in a private house for you.

Guideline prices, for a double room (two persons) per night in the high season, for hotels, at the time of writing, are: Copenhagen – lowest category (room without bathroom) Dkr 340–460; (room with bathroom) Dkr 450–875; medium category (room with bathroom) Dkr 770–995; highest category (room with bathroom) from Dkr 895. Provincial hotels – lowest category (room without bathroom) Dkr 225–350; (room with bathroom) Dkr 300–500; medium category (room without bathroom) Dkr 340–390; (room with bathroom) Dkr 490–595; highest category (room without bathroom) Dkr 375–595; (room with bathroom) from Dkr 570. In most cases breakfast will be included in the prices.

Most hotels offer substantial reductions out of the peak summer season. Reductions are also usual for children when they have extra beds in the parents' bedroom, while some hotels have family rooms.

Host and Guest Service in London can arrange comfortable accommodation in private homes. The accommodation is graded into three categories – budget, middle range and luxury. In 1993 the price per person was from £24.50 to £47.50 per night and where there are several persons there is a reduction. Their address is Harwood House, 27 Effie Road, London SW6 1EN. Tel: 071-731 5340.

HOTEL CHEQUES

There are several hotel cheque and voucher schemes available which can reduce the cost of accommodation and are ideally suited to the motorist. Best Western Hotels offer cheques which are valid from May 15 to September 9. Each cheque covers an overnight stay for one person in a double room with bathroom. Current cost is Dkr 320, although some hotels charge a supplement. Best Western have 30 hotels in Denmark.

Scandic, with 18 hotels, have their MiniPas which costs DKr 100 for a year and can be used from April 2–13, June 18 – August 16, October 15 – 25 and Fridays – Sundays all year. With the MiniPas the rate for a room (single, double or three or four bedded with bathroom) is DKr 595 per night and includes breakfast. Available from Scandic hotels or selected travel agents.

The ProSkandinavia Hotel Check System have vouchers which are valid for payment at 100 hotels all over Denmark. Each voucher costs £23 (1993) and two or three are needed to pay for a night's accommodation. Valid all year, subject to certain conditions. Available from Haman Scandinavia Ltd., Unit No.4, 4 Crawford Avenue, Wembley, Middx. HAO 2UU. Tel: 071–437 3439. Fax: 081–902 9894.

The Scandinavian Bonus Pass gives you a 15–20 per cent discount at the 19 InterDan hotels. Valid from May 15 to October 1 and all weekends. Obtainable from selected travel agents.

INN CHEQUES

Cheques are available for accommodation at 69 Danish inns. Each cheque is Dkr 375 for a single room or Dkr 535 for a double room with private bathroom and includes breakfast. At some inns a supplement of Dkr 100 is charged. There are special rates for children and special deals for families.

These cheques are administered by Dansk Kroferie, but details can be had from the DTB's London office.

Danish inns vary quite considerably and range from the old 'royal privilege' inns to modern ones which are really hotels. They can be small with only a few bedrooms to quite large establishments. Often the original old building has been enlarged with a modern extension, sometimes with motel style accommodation.

They are to be found in towns and villages, in the country or by the sea or by the roadside. Some are as expensive as the better hotels. There are still plenty of the really picturesque kind: half-timbered, thatched roof and with an interior stuffed with enough bygones to stock a fair sized antique shop.

The food they offer is invariably good, wholesome fare, while quite a number have a deservedly high reputation for the quality of their cuisine. In the latter you will pay accordingly. You can always just have tea or coffee or a soft drink at a *kro* and they do not have bars as in a British pub – drinks being served at your table.

Some inns are well-suited to anglers, being close to rivers or with rivers actually running through their grounds. At others you will find such amenities as a swimming pool or children's play area.

Approximate prices for bed and breakfast for a double room are Dkr 250–525. These rates will be a little higher for a room with a private bathroom – which is not always available.

SELF-CATERING

A development of the last 20 years has been the building of self-catering holiday hotels or holiday centres. A typical example consists of blocks of well-equipped apartments, each having its own kitchen, bathroom, living room and bedrooms and sleeping from two to nine persons. One building within the complex will have a range of amenities such as a restaurant or cafeteria, indoor or outdoor swimming pool, games room, sauna and solarium and children's play area. They are mostly by the sea, some being almost on the beach and, of course, they are ideally suited to family holidays. The later examples have got away from the 'barrack block' approach and have a host of activities available.

Prices vary quite widely, depending on the centre and the time of year. In the summer the minimum stay will be a week but out of season you can stay for shorter periods.

No service is provided and you will do your own cleaning, make your own beds and so on, but the price normally covers final cleaning of the apartment. In some cases the cost includes electricity and water heating and you can hire bed linen and towels if you don't want to take your own.

At Himmerland Golf and Country Club, for example, accommodation is in cottages for two to six persons. Facilities include 9-hole and 18-hole courses, indoor and outdoor pools, tennis courts, sauna, exercise room, table tennis, billiards, restaurant and bar. Activities range from riding to windsurfing.

Danland has seven self-catering holiday hotels which are all pretty big and by the sea. The designs vary but they are very typical of this type of accommodation. Among other holiday centres which have particularly attractive styles and locations and which do not feature large apartment blocks are Hotel Rudkøbing Skudehavn on the island of Langeland, Seven Islands near Ebeltoft in eastern Jutland and the Scandinavian Holiday Centre at Lemvig on Jutland's west coast.

FARMHOUSE HOLIDAYS

Over 25 years ago the Danes launched what proved to be one of their most successful holiday ideas – the farmhouse holiday. The concept was a great success and the farmhouse holiday continues to thrive and is one of the alternatives available to the visiting motorist.

There are two versions, one in which you stay on the farm as paying guests while on the other you cater for yourself in a separate apartment in the farmhouse or in a detached cottage nearby. All farms in the scheme are inspected by the local tourist association and one member of the farmer's family will be able to speak English.

When you are a paying guest you will usually take your meals with your Danish hosts and you will experience good, straightforward Danish cooking and be well fed. I have never yet heard anyone complain of anything except a certain amount of expansion around the waistline. You will be expected to keep your own bedroom(s) tidy, but that is the extent of your 'chores' although you are always welcome to help out it you want to.

Where you are catering for yourself everything will be provided except towels and bed linen and the apartment or cottage will include bedrooms, living room, kitchen and bathroom (with shower and toilet and hot and cold water).

Either version makes a good family holiday and they are very popular with children who regard the daily routine on the farm as extremely fascinating. In many cases the difficulty is trying to get them off the farm. The other bonus of the farmhouse holiday is that many guests make an enduring friendship with their hosts.

Farms offering accommodation will be found in most parts of Denmark and prices are standardised. At the time of writing the cost per person, per day is Dkr 230 (half board). There is a 50% reduction for children under 12 and a 75% reduction for children under four. The cost of the self-catering alternative is Dkr 1,900 for one week for an apartment sleeping four to six persons.

There is a very helpful brochure available (obtainable from the DTB) which among other things lists what animals are on the farm – right down to a rabbit and a duck!

SUMMERHOUSES

Summerhouses are a Scandinavian speciality. In Denmark you will find them all over the country with considerable variation in their style, size and situation. They are mostly privately owned, the owner using his summerhouse for part of the year and letting it for the remainder. Various organisations handle the letting arrangements, often through the local tourist office.

The extremely wide range of designs and their furnishing means that the letting charges also vary considerably. A lot depends on location – near the sea or in the country, by a lake or near a town. Standard equipment and services will include electricity, hot and cold water, refrigerator, cooker (but usually with only heating rings and no oven), shower and toilet.

Average size will be 540/650 sq ft and the interior will probably consist of a large open-plan living/dining room with the kitchenette at one end, bedrooms with bunk beds and the bathroom.

There are more luxurious ones available – each having their own indoor pool, sauna, solarium and whirlpool, the cost reflects these added features. Most of the tour operators specialising in Denmark offer summerhouse holidays as an inclusive package. Prices are much lower out of season – for example a typical one week arrangement would cost £134 per person in April or £221 in October but £322 in August. These rates include the ferry crossings from the UK to Denmark.

YOUTH HOSTELS

There are just over 100 youth and family hostels located throughout Denmark and they can be used by people of all ages and whether you are on foot, bicycle, motor cycle or car. Many of the hostels have small family rooms, usually sleeping two to six persons as well as dormitory style accommodation.

Beds are provided with blankets and pillows, but you need to bring your own bed linen or it can be hired at most hostels. Sleeping bags are not allowed.

The majority of hostels serve meals which are very reasonably priced and there are guest kitchens available if you want to do your own cooking. You bring your own plates and cutlery but kitchen utensils are provided.

An overnight stay costs (in 1993) Dkr 53–84 per person in a family room or Dkr 53 per person in a dormitory. Advance booking is recommended for families and is also essential during the period 1 September – 15 May. There are certain conditions relating to the time of arrival, etc. For overnight stays a valid membership card issued by the Youth Hostels Association in the UK is required but failing this an international youth hostel card, valid for a year, can be obtained in Denmark (cost approximately Dkr 112). Guest cards, valid for one night, are also available at a cost of Dkr 22.

The DTB in London has a helpful brochure covering both camping sites and youth and family hostels.

The hostel buildings range from former manor houses to small cottages or modern purpose-built units. Interiors tend to be up-to-date while some of them have a swimming pool. An increasing number have special facilities for the disabled.

CAMPING

Denmark probably has more camping sites for its area than anywhere else. There are over 500 approved sites to choose from and many of them occupy extremely scenic and well-landscaped settings. Apart from accommodating visitors with tents or caravans, some sites also have overnight cabins.

The Danish Camping Council inspects all sites at regular intervals and without prior warning, and they are placed in one-star, two-star or three-star categories. Minimum requirements are acceptable sanitary installations, drinking water and suitable ground. A two-star site must have showers, razor points, laundry and ironing facilities and a provision store not more than 1 km away. Three-star sites have to meet even higher standards. Many sites are well arranged with different areas screened by trees or hedges. They often occupy positions of considerable natural beauty. The better sites include a small supermarket and quite a few now have swimming pools and children's play areas.

A detailed guide to approved sites is published each year by the Danish Camping Council and can be obtained from *Campingrådet*, Hessrløgade 16, DK-2100 Copenhagen Ø, price Dkr 100 by mail. As already mentioned the DTB in London has a useful brochure listing the sites.

At approved sites visitors should have an International Camping Carnet. This can be issued at the first site at which you stay.

Continued on page 41

A typical whitewashed Danish church nestles amongst the trees with its tower overlooking the beautiful Svendborg Sound.

With only the fairytale princess missing , Tranekær Castle makes an impressive sight. It is on the island of Langeland.

ABOVE - There are more colourful houses in Aerøskøbing, on the island of Aerø, than probably anywhere else in Denmark. This is just one of the cobbled streets in this idyllic little town.

BELOW - Denmark's biggest attraction for children is Legoland at Billund on Jutland. Everything is there from a wild west town to Piratland.

Denmark has some of the finest sandy beaches in Europe. One of the best areas to find them is on Jutland's north-west coast and what's more they are seldom crowded.

ABOVE - As soon as the sun shines the Danes go out of doors. Outdoor cafes are popular. This the Cafe Kultorvet in the heart of Copenhagen.

BELOW - The most popular attraction in Denmark is Tivoli Gardens in the heart of Copenhagen which in 1993 celebrated its 150th anniversary.

ABOVE - Picturesque Nyhavn in Copenhagen. Once the haunt of sailors and full of bars, it is now much more trendy with pavement cafes and excellent restaurants.

BELOW - The impressive interior of Roskilde Cathedral - the Danish equivalent of Westminster Abbey

ABOVE - The Danes were pioneers in the creation of pedestrianised streets. This one is in the pleasant south Jutland town of Haderslev.

BELOW - Inside the Hans Christian Andersen museum in Odense, his birthplace on the island of Funen. The museum includes many of his personal belongings.

The Old Town (Den Gamle By) in Århus is a wonderful collection of over 60 17th and 18th century buildings from all over Denmark.

Overnight prices depend on the site facilities but a typical charge for two adults and one child at a one star site is Dkr 80 rising to Dkr 100 at a three star site (1993 prices).

The Danish motoring organisation FDM also runs some 20 sites and these are open to foreign visitors holding an International Camping Carnet.

Camping at places other than designated sites in a tent, car or caravan is not allowed without the landowner's permission. Nor is it permitted to camp in car parks or lay-bys and strong measures are taken against anyone camping on sand dunes or the beach – offenders being fined on the spot.

FACILITIES FOR THE HANDICAPPED

Denmark, like its Scandinavian neighbours, has paid a great deal of attention to the needs of the disabled. There are numerous hotels which can accommodate the handicapped and some of the holiday centres have apartments with special facilities for the disabled. This also applies to Danish youth and family hostels.

The Danish Tourist Board has a really excellent 98-page Travel Guide for the Disabled which is full of clear, practical information – including travel by car, accommodation, eating places, bathing, theatres and sights. Recommended.

FOOD AND DRINK

ONE OF THE pleasures of a holiday abroad should be the food, and in Denmark there is ample opportunity to enjoy the country's culinary specialities. The Danes are enthusiastic about food and therefore they pay a lot of attention to its preparation and serving.

Although mass production has made inroads in the catering field, just as in other countries, nevertheless there is still plenty of individuality and many dishes reflect the character of the country and its geographical position.

The raw materials that form the basis of Danish cuisine are, first and foremost, fish and shellfish, followed by meat, dairy products, vegetables and fruit. Many dishes are comparatively simple – in fact simplicity is the keynote – but because of the freshness of the raw materials they triumph. They take a lot of care with the table arrangements and the presentation of the dishes so that they are pleasing to the eye as well as exciting to the palate.

You only have to see a table prepared for some party or gala dinner to get the full measure of this art of presentation. It need not be a great event at some expensive restaurant in the capital; I have seen a table laid for a wedding party at a country inn and another, at a small seaside hotel, prepared for a local dinner and in both cases the table arrangements were a joy to behold. They only awaited the colour and animation of the guests and good food and drink to complete the picture.

Danish restaurateurs – at least many of them – believe that whatever the price of the dish it should involve the best ingredients. So you can always order a cheaper dish and know that the quality will be maintained. There have been very few occasions when I have been offered anything below par. On the other hand I have visited several small restaurants where I did not expect to eat particularly well and have been surprised and delighted at the food presented to me.

OPEN SANDWICHES

The two best known elements of Danish cuisine are the open sandwich (*smørrebrød*) and the cold table (*Det Koldt Bord*). The most minor part of the open sandwich is the piece of bread and butter which forms the base. This may be white bread (*franskbrød*) or rye bread (*rugbrød*) and on top will be either fish, meat or cheese with salad, dressings or garnishes. The popular ones are herring (it may be marinated, pickled or in a curry sauce), roast beef, pork, ham, salami, liver paste, egg, fish (a small fish fillet), shrimps and cheese. All will be carefully garnished. Two open sandwiches will prove quite filling and if that isn't enough you can always have another one.

Smørrebrød is one of the best solutions for lunch: not too much and not too little and you determine how much you want either on the basis of quantity or price. (The cost of a sandwich varies from DKr 15 to Dkr 45). You may think that some of them are expensive but when you see what has been artistically balanced on that little piece of bread you will realise they are good value. Obviously the more expensive ones are those with toppings of such things as fresh shrimps or smoked salmon.

Open sandwiches are a Danish institution and something you must try on your visit and nearly all restaurants and cafeterias offer them. In many cases you will be brought a long printed list and you mark on it the sandwiches you want, although this practice does seem to be dying out.

With your open sandwiches you can drink beer, and possibly have an aquavit (it goes particularly well with herring and the Danes say it gives the fish something in which to swim!). Or you can have soft drinks, or tea or coffee.

THE COLD TABLE

Basically the cold table is a help-yourself buffet with a wide variety of hot and cold dishes: fish, meat, vegetables, salads and garnishes plus sweets, cheese and fruit. But this is reducing it to a very prosaic level because when you see a really well presented cold table it is a mouth-watering work of art. Compared with a few years ago there are not so many restaurants offering this speciality and this may be due to people being more calorie conscious. You pay a fixed price and then help yourself to whatever you want – and, of course, as much as you want. Beer (plus aquavit for the herring) or soft drinks are the beverages to go with it.

There is an order of things when taking the cold table and you do not heap one plate willy-nilly with a glorious mixture. No, that is not the way to do it. You start with the herring, which is really the appetiser, then you can look at the other fish or maybe some Danish caviar. Then back to the table for another clean plate (use one for each 'course' – after all you aren't doing the washing up) and sample some cold meat with a salad or perhaps try the hot food. Then there is the delicious dessert (leave room for that) and conclude with some good Danish cheese and perhaps a little fruit. Finally, a cup of coffee and you are replete.

BREAKFAST

In nearly all hotels breakfast is now a help-yourself buffet. There is usually fruit juice and milk, cereal and oatmeal, a variety of rolls and bread, jam and marmalade, cheese and cold meat and tea or coffee. The more elaborate include a wider variety of meats, liver paste, herring, boiled eggs and Danish pastries. A small point: there is sometimes sour milk (buttermilk) as well as ordinary milk on the breakfast buffet. Don't confuse the two as it could add an unusual taste to your cornflakes.

FOOD AND DRINK

SOME DANISH DISHES

Fish Fish dishes are the outstanding experience, being so fresh and of such high quality. Plaice is the basic fish, served steamed, fried in oil or butter 'a la meuniere' and garnished with vegetables and shellfish. Eel is another speciality which you can have fried with creamed potatoes and a white sauce or boiled with rice and a curry sauce. Shellfish are also splendid: lobsters, shrimps, mussels and oysters are all of exceptionally good quality. Equally good is the smoked salmon – the best comes from the island of Bornholm – served in fine slices with *surbrød* (bread made from rye meal and caraway seeds) or with spinach, scrambled egg or asparagus. Also the Scandinavian speciality called *Gravad laks* – salmon marinated with salt, sugar and dill and served with *surbrød* and a cold sauce of oil, mustard and sugar sprinkled with chopped dill.

Meat Danish meat is home-produced and of good quality although by contrast the bacon is nowhere near as good as that which is exported to the UK. A dish you will find on many menus is *Frikadeller* – a type of meat ball or rissole and made from freshly minced pork or pork and veal, flour, egg, salt, pepper and grated onions. It is often served with red cabbage, boiled potatoes and a thick brown gravy. It may not sound that exciting but it tastes delicious. Beef, pork and veal dishes are all good while lamb is more popular now than it was a few years ago. Poultry is usually either chicken or duck, while game is available in season.

Cheese There are quite a few domestic cheeses, apart from the widely known Danish blue (*Danablu*). They include *Castello* (white-veined), *Blå Castello* (blue-veined), *Mycella*, *Esrom*, *Danbo*, *Maribo*, *Havarti* and *Samsø* (all hard cheeses).

WHERE TO EAT AND DRINK

Places to eat and drink fall into different categories. Here are some of them:

Bar	Drinks of all kinds, including beer, wine and spirits.
Bistro	Usually a place for inexpensive meals of all kinds.
Bodega	Drinks but also serving light meals.
Cafe	Drinks and often light meals. Some are comparable to restaurants.
Cafeteria	Inexpensive self-service establishments offering simple hot and cold dishes, open sandwiches, etc., tea and coffee and various kinds of drinks.
Fiskerestaurant	Specialises in seafood but probably having some meat dishes on the menu.

Frokostrestaurant/ Frokoststue	Open sandwiches and small hot dishes.
Grillbar	Grilled beef, chicken, sausages, etc.
Hotel	Restaurants usually cover all meals from breakfast to late night snacks.
Konditori	Pastries and cakes, tea, coffee and soft drinks.
Kro	Inn, providing all kinds of food and drinks (may close on one day a week).
Motel	Facilities can vary from a bar, with possibly some light snacks, to a full-scale restaurant.
Pub	Drinks with a greater emphasis on beer, and light meals such as open sandwiches.
Pølsevogn	A hamburger stand or kiosk, often found in a town square or similar location. Frankfurters and hamburgers.
Restaurant	All kinds of food and drinks.
Smørrebrødsforretning	Basically a take-away for open sandwiches. Frequently sells soft drinks. Quite often you can consume your sandwiches on the premises at a stand-up counter. Some of them keep open late and may have an automat outside for when they are closed.

Besides Danish restaurants there is a growing number of speciality restaurants offering the cuisine of other countries, such as French, Italian, Indian and Chinese. Pizzerias have become very common and there are the inevitable burger bars and the equally inevitable Macdonalds.

Opening hours vary but in general, restaurants are open from 12 noon to midnight (last orders for hot dishes normally 9.00 p.m. or 10.00 p.m.).

There are now many restaurants which serve food for diabetics – look for the sign at the entrance with a smiling chef and the words: 'Diebetes mad – sund mad for alle' (Food for diabetics – healthy food for everyone').

DRINKS

Domestically produced alcoholic drinks include aquavit (schnapps), beer and liqueurs. There are different kinds of aquavit, some of which are flavoured with sweet myrtle, caraway or dill. They vary from being colourless to being pale gold but are always served well chilled.

Among the liqueurs the best known to the UK visitor is Peter

FOOD AND DRINK

Heering's cherry brandy, but there are others flavoured with coffee or blackcurrant for example. Then there are the bitters, the most widely drunk being *Gammel Dansk* which has the reputation for being a good hangover remedy.

The lightest beer, with the lowest alcohol content, is *Lys pilsner* while lagers are referred to as either pilsner or lager (but more probably by the brand name, such as *Carlsberg Hof* or *Tuborg Grøn*). A stronger lager is *Eksport* or *Guldøl*, while draught beer is *fadøl* and in case you have not realised it already, the word for beer is *øl*. Stout is called *porter*.

Of course there is a considerable difference between the price you will pay for a bottle of beer in a supermarket and what it will cost when served to you in a restaurant. The much higher price of the latter reflects the cost of labour, plus VAT and service.

Wines are principally imported from France, Germany, Italy and Spain. *Åben vin*, *bordvin* or *husetsvin* stand for open, table and house wine respectively, and all basically describe a restaurant's house wine. Usually of a good standard it is more often presented in the bottle rather than a carafe (when it may be referred to as *karaffelvin*). Wine lists will have a good selection of better wines but with prices to match. Types of wine are *Rosevin* – rosé, *rødvin* – red and *hvidvin* – white.

USEFUL TRANSLATIONS

Non-Alcoholic drinks

Appelsin	orangeade
Cacao	chocolate
Citronvand	lemon soda
Dansk Vand	plain soda water
Kaffe	coffee
Kærnemælk	buttermilk
Letmælk	low fat milk
Mineralvand	mineral water/soda water
Mælk	milk
Skummetmælk	skim milk
Sødmælk	milk*
Te	tea
Tomatjuice	tomato juice
Vand	water
Æblemost	apple juice

*There are various kinds of cartoned milk, but this is the standard one for drinking, putting on your cereal or in your tea.

Menu terms

Børnemenu	children's menu
Dagens middag	set dinner
Dagens ret	dish of the day
Dampet	steamed

Desserter	desserts
Farseret/fyldt	stuffed
Fisk	fish
Filet	fillet (meat or fish)
Fjerkræ	poultry
Forretter	starter
Frisk	fresh
Friteret	deep fried
Frokost	lunch
Frugt	fruit
Gratineret	au gratin
Grillretter	grill dishes
Grillstegt	grilled
Grønsager	vegetables
Hovedretter	main dishes
Kogt	boiled
Kold	cold
Koldt Bord	cold table – help-yourself buffet
Kød	meat (dishes)
Mad	food
Mellemretter	side dishes
Morgenmad/	breakfast
Morgencomplet	
Nat mad	late night snack
Osteanretning	cheeses
Pandestegt	cooked in a frying pan
Platte	a mini-cold table served on one large dish
Pocheret	poached
Salater	salads
Smørrebrød	open sandwiches
Snitter	mini-open sandwiches – more like canapés
Steg	roast
Supper	soups
Varme retter	hot dishes

Food terms – fish and shellfish

Ferskrøget laks	lightly smoked salmon
Fiskeboller	fish balls
Forel	trout
Gravad laks	salmon marinated in salt, sugar and dill
Hellefisk	flounder
Helleflynder	halibut
Hummer	lobster
Jomfruhummer	Norwegian crayfish/scampi
Karry sild	herring in curry sauce
Krabbe	crab

47

FOOD AND DRINK

Kryddersild	spiced pickled herring
Kuller	haddock
Laks	salmon
Marineret sild	marinated herring
Muslinger	mussels
Rejer	shrimps
Rødspætte	plaice
Rødtunge	lemon sole
Røget laks	smoked salmon
Sild	herring
Skaldyr	shellfish
Søtunge	sole
Østers	oysters
Ål	eel

Meat

Bajerske pølser	frankfurters/hot dogs
Bøf	beef steak
Crepinetter	pork or veal burgers
Engelsk bøf	steak and onions
Flæsk	pork
Fransk bøf	steak with parsley butter
Frikadeller	fried meatballs of pork or pork and veal
Grill pølse	grilled sausage
Hakkebøf	Danish-style beefburger
Helstegt højreb	roast saddle of beef
Helstegt lammeryg	roast saddle of lamb
Helstegt svinekam	roast loin of pork
Højrebskotelet	cutlet of prime rib of beef
Kalve filet	fillet of veal
Kødboller	meat balls
Lam	lamb
Lammekoteletter	lamb chops
Oksefilet	fillet of beef
Okseteg	roast beef
Pariserbøf	ground steak, lightly grilled both sides
Pølse	sausage
Ribbenssteg	roast rib of pork
Skinke	ham
Spegepølse	Danish salami

Poultry and Game

And	duck
Due	pigeon
Fasan	pheasant
Gås	goose
Høne	chicken (boiling fowl)
Kylling	chicken
Vildt	game

Cheese, eggs and cream

Blødkogt æg	soft boiled egg
Fløde	cream
Flødeskum	whipped cream
Hardkogt æg	hard boiled egg
Ost	cheese
Spejlæg	fried egg
Æg	egg
Æggekage	pan omelette
Røræg	scrambled egg

Vegetables

Agurk	cucumber
Asparges	asparagus
Bagt kartoffel	baked potato
Blomkål	cauliflower
Brasede kartofler/ Brasekartofler	saute potatoes
Bønner	beans
Franske kartofler	French fried potatoes
Grønkal	kale
Grønne æeter/Grønærter	peas
Gulerod/Gulerødder	carrots
Hvide kartofler	boiled potatoes
Hvidkål	white cabbage
Kartofler	potatoes
Løg	onion
Persille	parsley
Rosenkål	Brussels sprouts
Rødkål	red cabbage
Spinat	spinach
Surkål	sauerkraut
Ærter	peas

Fruit

Ananas	pineapple
Blommer	plum
Citron	lemon
Druer	grapes
Fersken	peach
Hindbær	raspberry
Jordbær	strawberry
Kirsebær	cherry
Nødder	nut
Pære	pear
Æble	apple

Various

Brød	bread

FOOD AND DRINK

Butterdej	puff pastry
Flute	dinner roll
Franskbrød	white bread
Kager	cakes and pastries
Kiks	biscuits
Pandekager	pancakes
Postej	pâté
Ris	rice
Ristet brød	toast
Rugbrød	rye bread
Sennep	mustard
Smør	butter
Sukker	sugar
Vafler	waffle
Wienerbrød	Danish pastry

Selected dishes

Biksemad	fried sliced onion, meat and potatoes
Brændende Kærlighed	mashed potato with fried bacon and onions
Flæsekæggekage	pan omelette with bacon
Høkerpande	fried onion, meat, liver, kidney and potatoes
Lobescowes	stew of beef and potatoes
Skipperlabskous	Captain's stew – a traditional thick stew

SHOPPING

DENMARK IS a good country in which to shop, not because things are cheap, but because of the range of products and the fact that the Danes are very design and quality conscious. There are the traditional goods for which Denmark has a deservedly high reputation: porcelain and glass, silverware and pewter, jewellery, furniture and furs. But apart from these, there are other products which are worthy of attention.

So what should the visitor look for? There are those traditional products already mentioned, although in most cases you will want to rule out furniture (too bulky) or furs (unless you have a very deep pocket). Porcelain, glass, silverware and pewter – the Danes call it tin – need not be the designs produced by the top names (with prices to match). There are plenty of really stunning examples available in the lower price ranges. Jewellery – gold, silver and also incorporating precious and semi-precious stones – is very attractive and includes some beautiful work by gifted designers and craftsmen. You will find a remarkably wide range, even in small-town jewellers.

Other products worth looking into include leather (expensive, but good), knitwear (especially woollen sweaters), toys (think of Lego, that's Danish), textiles, ceramics and needlework. It is a good country in which to find things for the home or garden. Merchandise for the home includes both pretty things and those of a more utilitarian nature.

The Danes love candles and they come in all shapes and sizes and are a good buy. This also applies to attractive candle holders and table decorations. Ironmongery, tools and garden equipment are worth looking at, although some brands will be familiar.

Denmark has become something of an international fashion centre in recent years and this is reflected in the ladies wear available (especially casual clothes for the young). Some of the exciting designs are very competitively priced. Chocolate and confectionary shops offer mouth-watering and tempting goodies, which may not be cheap but will be of excellent quality.

What is enjoyable is that even quite small towns have an attractive range of shops, with a wide selection of beautifully displayed merchandise. As shops are nearly all individually-owned the monotony of high streets filled with multiples is avoided. With many towns having pedestrian precincts, shopping or just browsing is very pleasant.

There are no chain stores as we know them, except among supermarkets. There are also comparatively few department stores, these being restricted to the larger towns and Copenhagen. What has grown in recent years has been the building of major shopping centres on the outskirts of the larger towns and cities (although even smaller towns are joining this trend). Taking Århus as an example, there is, on the outskirts, *City Vest* which incorporates two department stores and 62 specialist shops and

51

Bilka, a discount centre which has 32 shops and a cafeteria. In the city there are two major department stores: *Salling* which has 34 departments on six floors, and a branch of *Magasin*, which is the biggest department store in Copenhagen and also has branches in Ålborg, Odense, Lyngby and Rødovre. On the outskirts of Odense is Rosengårdcentret with 97 individual shops and the Obs department store all under one roof. Outside there is parking for 2,400 vehicles.

Driving around the countryside it will become apparent that there are many artists' workshops: painters, sculptors, potters and so on. Visiting them can be rewarding the key being whether you like their style and prices. There are plenty of antique and bric-à-brac shops in towns and villages and some of these may have items to interest you, depending on what you collect. Unfortunately you have less chance of finding a real bargain these days.

If Danish food has appealed to you then you should include a last minute call at a food shop or supermarket before you catch your ferry to Britain. For example, what about some jars of herring, or Danish caviar or cheese. There are several supermarket chains, including *Føtex, Brugsen, Irma* and *Qvickly*.

Supermarkets are well laid out, scrupulously clean and often include a cafeteria and toilets. Parking will be close at hand. The big ones include other merchandise besides food and drink.

SHOPPING IN COPENHAGEN

For the visitor, shopping in the Danish capital tends to be concentrated on *Strøget*, the long pedestrian street that runs from the Town Hall Square to Kongens Nytorv. It is in fact five streets which just run into each other. Along Strøget you will find the top shops and famous names: Georg Jensen, Royal Copenhagen Porcelain, Bing and Grøndahl and Illum – which has six floors and a superb range of merchandise. But there are many smaller stores and good specialist shops and plenty of small boutiques stocked with exciting new fashions.

You should explore the smaller streets and squares leading off Strøget where you will find shops and boutiques full of new ideas and designs. In the streets towards the university quarter (and not far from Strøget) are secondhand and antiquarian bookshops, stamp dealers and antique shops. There are two other pedestrian streets worth a browse: Købmagergade and Fiolstræde.

On *Kongens Nytorv* is Magasin, the capital's biggest department store which has a useful gift department if you get stuck for ideas and are short of time.

Credit cards are widely accepted. You can also pay in most shops by Eurocheque or travellers' cheque. If you want cash, the banks are open from 9.30 a.m. to 4.00 p.m. Mondays to Fridays

(6.00 p.m. on Thursdays) and are closed Saturdays, Sundays and bank holidays.

Shopping hours are usually 9.00 a.m. to 5.30 p.m. with late night shopping (9.00 a.m. to 7.00 p.m. or 8.00 p.m.) on Fridays. On Saturdays shops close at 1.00 p.m. (department stores at 2.00 p.m.). On the first Saturday of the month most shops remain open until 4.00 p.m. or 5.00 p.m. Some shops, particularly food shops, may close on Mondays. Outside normal hours you will find places open for the sale of tobacco, newspapers and confectionery. Bakeries, florists and *smørrebrødsforretning* (open sandwich take-aways) stay open for longer hours (bakers also open on Sundays). Some supermarkets have two late night openings a week, such as Thursdays to 7.00 p.m. and Fridays to 8.00 p.m. At the railway stations at Copenhagen, Århus and Ålborg there are supermarkets open every day of the week and the station kiosks stay open late in the evenings.

Danish shopkeepers have sales just like anywhere else and this may provide the opportunity to pick up a bargain. Look for the word *Udsalg* and then see what is on offer.

SHOPPING FOR FOOD

If you are self-catering or want to have picnics then you will need food. This presents no great problem and the easiest solution is undoubtedly the supermarket, either one of the major ones in a town or one of the mini-markets which will be found in villages. The larger supermarkets will have fresh food counters as well as packaged and frozen food. Most places seem to be able to find someone who has a few words of English if you get into difficulties, although sign language can achieve wonders. Instructions on packets pose more of a problem as misinterpretation could mean the difference between a good meal and a culinary disaster. Bakers provide a splendid range of bread, rolls and cakes and pastries, all deliciously fresh and appetising.

The open sandwich take-aways can solve the picnic problem in an instant. Just select the ones you want and you will get them neatly boxed. If a filling (or perhaps it should be called topping on an open sandwich) is not on display they can usually make it up for you. Many sandwich shops also sell soft drinks.

If you think you may be indulging in picnics remember to take some knives and forks (even plastic ones will do) as trying to eat open sandwiches in your fingers can be a messy business. A cold bag is also useful, although these and other picnic equipment will be found in profusion in Denmark.

There are lots of spacious lay-bys and pleasant areas for picnics. Quite a few have toilets and they nearly all have litter bins or sacks.

ATTRACTIONS FOR CHILDREN AND ADULTS

IN SPITE OF its modest size Denmark is overflowing with things to see and do. There are the simple visual pleasures of the scenery: the forests, the varied coastline, the lakes and rivers. History provides a subject for many more attractions, ranging from the pre-historic, through the Viking era and the Middle Ages to more recent times.

The country is rich in castles and manor houses. The former are less forbidding and fortress-like than those found in Britain, but they are often impressive architecturally and are invariably sited in beautiful surroundings. Many are open to the public displaying their treasures for all to see.

Museums abound, and these are not dry-as-dust affairs but places that really bring the past to life through the imaginative treatment of their exhibits. The Danes are experts in the creation of outdoor museums with old buildings painstakingly restored and re-erected on suitable sites. Of course the Vikings play an important part in the attractions of historic interest, but other times also receive their fair share of attention. There are superb art galleries with impressive Danish and international collections while specialist musuems cover subjects as varied as drifting sands and ships in bottles.

Architecture plays its part in things to see, as a great deal of pleasure can be gained from the impressive modern designs as well as strolling round carefully preserved old buildings and streets which have received an enormous amount of care and attention.

Denmark is very much a children's country, so it is no surprise that the two most popular attractions are Legoland and the Tivoli Gardens. But there are so many other sights and scenes that appeal to the younger visitor, from the simple (like a sandy beach) to the more mechanical (such as a veteran steam train).

A particularly popular attraction is the Sommerland. These are individually owned activity parks where you pay an admission fee and then your children are free to use all the facilities on offer as many times as they like. Sommerlands have all sorts of things from trampolines to aerial cableways – many of them of considerable ingenuity while some of them have added extensive aquaparks which are very popular. They are all well supervised, kept remarkably clean and tidy and have good catering facilities – or you are welcome to take your own picnic (you can even use their barbecues). For children they are wonderful, even if they are not quite as much fun for adults, but they do make a good, reasonably priced day out for the family.

In this chapter I include a broad range of attractions, but there are many, many more and some of these are referred to in the individual itineraries. In most cases I have given an indication of when museums, etc., are open, but I must emphasise that these may change from season to season.

Check with the Danish Tourist Board's London office or with the appropriate local tourist office. Remember that many attractions may have very restricted opening hours out of the main summer season – or may, in fact, be closed. Danish museums have inclined towards very limited opening times although they have improved just recently.

Expect to pay an entrance fee at virtually all museums, castles and so on but there will be reduced prices for children and probably for students and senior citizens. Parking is always free and you can expect to find clean toilets; if catering facilities are provided these will be hygienic and inviting.

The entries in this chapter are arranged geographically, i.e. Jutland, Funen, Zealand, etc. In the case of Jutland I have started in the south near the German frontier and progressed to the northern tip. Those places marked with a ☆ should interest children, while the numbers identify the attractions on the accompanying map.

JUTLAND

1 Frøslev, near Padborg An internment camp for Danes in World War 2, now restored as a museum and memorial to those who were imprisoned. Open daily, except Mons.

2 Tønder Former centre of the lace-making industry. Well-preserved 17th-18th century townscape. Excellent museum on the cultural history of the town with collections of lace, silverware and pottery. Open daily, except Mons. 16th century church.

3 Møgeltønder Has a beautifully preserved cobbled village street, lined with lime trees which runs from the church at one end to Schackenborg Palace at the other.

4 Dybbøl Banke, near Sønderborg Associated with the Danish-German war of 1864 and now a national monument. Dybbøl Banke centre. Open daily, Apr–Oct. The restored Dybbøl wind-mill is a national symbol and has a small museum.

5 Sønderborg A busy town on the island of Als (a bridge away from Jutland). Imposing castle from 1150 with Renaissance chapel and baronial hall. It now houses the museum of South Jutland. Open daily.

6 Løgumkloster Church built by Cistercian monks in the 14th century. Has the largest carillon in Scandinavia. Open to the public.

7 Åbenrå The most interesting thing in this town is the museum with its very good maritime section and ship models. Open daily, except Mons.

8 Haderslev Majestic cathedral from 1621, the tallest church in Scandinavia. Museum of local history with an open air display of buildings. Open June-end Aug, closed Mons. Schleswig Carriage Collection (*Slesvigske Vognsamling*) – carriages and sleighs from 1870–1930. Open mid-June – mid-Aug.

9 Christiansfeld Founded in 1773 by the Moravian Brethren who built a small town with a simple but completely harmonious architectural style. Museum. Church, with plain whitewashed interior and no altar or pulpit, can hold 1,000 worshippers. Skamlingsbanken, eight miles from Christiansfeld, is a national monument with fine views of the countryside.

10 Rømø Island off the west coast of Jutland reached by a six-mile causeway – see chapter on the smaller islands, page 139.

11 Ribe Denmark's oldest market town with a unique historical atmosphere and beautifully preserved buildings and streets. Splendid five-aisled cathedral. Access to the tower at certain times (234 steps to the top). Hans Tausen's House – residence of the Bishop of Ribe in 1541 – now an archeological museum. *Quedern's Gård*, merchant's house, c. 1580, now a very interesting museum of interiors. Open daily, except Mons. Ribe Art Museum (Ribe Kunstmuseum) has an interesting collection of 19th and early 19th century Danish paintings. Open daily (mid-Sept–mid-June closed Mons).

12 Mandø Small island off the Jutland coast which can be reached at low tide by 'tractor bus'. Little church and museum.

13 Jels Orion Planetarium and Observatory (opened July 1993). Exhibitions of astronomy and space travel. ☆ Open daily, not Weds Sept–June.

14 Fanø Island facing Esbjerg. Eleven miles long, reached by ferry (20 mins). Superb beaches on the west coast. Distinctive seaman's church (*Nordby Kirke*) with ship models. Fanø museum in a former seaman's home is full of interesting little exhibits. Open summer only. Shipping and Costume Museum (*Fanø Søfarts og Dragtudstilling*) at Nordby is also worth visiting. Open daily, except Suns Oct–Apr. Hannes Hus at Sønderho is a typical island home of the 19th c. Limited summer opening hours.

15 Esbjerg Busy port of entry from UK. Fisheries and Maritime Museum (*Fiskeri og Søfarts Museet*)☆ has a unique collection of fishing gear, models and also full-size outdoor exhibits. The saltwater aquarium has 200 species of fish and there is an adjoining sealarium. Open all year. Esbjerg Museum – history of the town. Open daily, closed Mons. Printing Museum (*Bogtrykmuseet*). Open daily, closed Mons. Old lightship moored by Fanø dock, now a museum. Open daily May–Oct. Art Pavilion – collection of contemporary Danish art. Open all year.

16 Varde Sommerland – amusement and activity park.☆ Has 40 activities. Open mid-May – early Sept. Varde Miniby ☆ – the town in miniature as it was in 1800. Artillery Museum (*Artillerimuseet*) – history of artillery from the Middle Ages. Open all year. Museum of cultural history.

17 Kolding Koldinghus Castle was a royal residence for centuries. Set on fire in 1808 and under restoration since 1900. Newly restored wings are splendid. Open all year. Geographical Garden (*Den geografiske Have*) – has more than 2,000 species of trees and plants. Open all year, Kunstmuseet Trapholt – a 20th century art museum in lovely surroundings by the Kolding Fjord. Open daily.

18 Vejle Attractive fjord location. The southern arm is particularly beautiful and rises steeply through beech woods (321 ft above sea level) to Munkebjerg. Vejle Art Museum (*Vejle Kunstmuseum*) has the main emphasis on modernism and neo-surrealism. Open daily, closed Mons. Vejle Museum is in two parts, one being a 19th century merchant's house and illustrates the history of the town. Open daily (not Mons, Suns Nov–Mar).

19 Jelling Ancient seat of Danish royalty. King Gorm the Old and Queen Thyre are believed to be buried in one of two huge burial mounds. Church has 12th century frescoes and ancient runic stones in the churchyard.

20 Givskud Lions Park (*Løveparken*).☆ Safari park with 700 animals. Open daily, late June-late Oct.

21 Billund Legoland.☆ Second biggest attraction in Denmark. Fantastic models in landscaped surroundings made from millions of Lego bricks. All kinds of rides and things to do – from digging for gold to enjoying the wild west town of Legoredo. Open daily, 1 May – 19 Sept. Center Mobilium.☆ A modern building housing three museums: Danish Automobile Museum, Danish Aircraft Museum and the Falck Museum (rescue and salvage vehicles). Open daily, except Mons.

22 Grindsted Occupation Collection (*Besættelsessamlingen*). Exhibits show the German occupation of Denmark in 1940–1945 and its affect on everyday life. Open Weds 7.00pm–8.00pm.

23 Glud Small village with an interesting museum of Danish rural life with many fascinating exhibits. Open daily, April–Sept.

24 Ringkøbing Market town six miles from the west coast. Attractive little streets and old buildings. Museum with archaeological and town historical collections. Open all year, daily in summer. At the local airport at Stauning is a museum with 35 veteran aircraft including Denmark's oldest plane in a flyable condition. Sommerland West,☆ about five miles north at Hee is an activity park covering 55 acres and with many activities. Open daily, 5 May–29 Aug.

ATTRACTIONS FOR CHILDREN
AND ADULTS

25 Thorsminde *Strandingsmuseet St. George*. Museum consisting mainly of articles salvaged from the British flagship St. George which foundered in 1811 with the loss of 1,300 lives. Open daily, early Apr–late Oct. Open Sats and Suns at other times.

26 Holstebro Impressive range of sculptures and fountains in different parts of the town. Holstebro Museum – a new and impressive museum with a wide variety of exhibits. Open daily in summer, otherwise closed Mons. Holstebro Art Museum has modern Danish and foreign collections. Open daily in summer, otherwise closed Mons.

27 Herning Modern commercial town with impressive modern art museum and sculpture park. Open daily, except Mons. Herning Museum which includes an appealing series of little dioramas depicting rural life in the past. The open air section includes Danish rare breeds. Open daily in July, otherwise daily except Mons.

28 Silkeborg Town in the centre of the Danish lake district. Museum in the town's oldest building, includes the preserved head of the Tollund Man – over 2,000 years old.☆ Open daily Apr–Oct (Wed, Sat, Sun Nov–Mar). Art Museum features modern European works. Open daily, except Mons. Aqua☆ – aquarium and museum – fish, birds, animals and plants. Open daily. 1861 paddle steamer '*Hjejlen*' provides lake trips in summer. Surrounding scenery includes Himmelbjerget ('*Heavenly Mountain*') 426ft above sea level.

29 Bryrup-Vrads Preserved railway runs through delightful countryside between these two points. ☆ Weekends in summer.

30 Gjern Jutland Car Museum (*Jysk Automobil Museum*).☆ An interesting and expanding collection of over 130 beautifully restored old motor vehicles. Open daily in summer, weekends spring and autumn.

31 Mønsted Kalkgruber ☆ World's largest underground limestone caverns with 25 miles of galleries. Bat museum. Open daily mid-May – mid-Sept, except Mons (daily end-June – mid-Sept).

32 Viborg Cathedral in Romanesque style, founded 1130. Present building dates from 1876 and has impressive murals. Pleasant park by lake. Viborg Museum (*Viborg Stiftsmuseum*) features the history of the citizens of the town from the first hunters until the present day. Open daily Jun–end Aug, otherwise closed Mons.

33 Århus Denmark's second largest city. The Old Town (*Den Gamle By*)☆ is a fascinating collection of over 60 17th and 18th century buildings – houses, shops, workshops, etc. from all over Denmark. Open all year. Museum of pre-history, Moesgård (*Forhistorisk Museum*) occupies a delightful setting between woods and water. Open daily, closed Mons in winter. *Domkirke* – late Gothic cathedral and longest church in Denmark. *Musikhuset* – superb modern concert hall with several stages, cafe and restaurant. *Århus Kunstmuseum* has a fine collection of 18th and 19th century paintings from Denmark's 'golden age' plus modern art. Open daily, except Mons. Danish Fire Brigade Museum (*Det Danske Brandværnsmuseum*).☆ Biggest collection of fire fighting appliances in the world (over 80 fire engines). Open daily, Apr–Oct. Tivoli Friheden.☆ Amusement park with, among other things, the biggest roller-coaster and oldest roundabout in Denmark. Open daily, 1 May–15 Aug. *Kvindemuseet* – the Women's Museum – devoted to Danish women's cultural history. Open daily, except Mons (1 June – 31 July open daily). Århus Aquarium, Tranbjerg.☆ Rare fish from all over the world. Open all year. Marselisborg Forest and Deer Park – a beautiful area on the edge of the city and by the water.

34 Samsø Pretty island between east Jutland and Zealand – see The Smaller Islands, page 139.

35 Ebeltoft Attractive small town and popular holiday centre. Frigate '*Jylland*'.☆ The oldest preserved wooden ship in Denmark. Open daily in summer, Sats, Suns at other times. Ebeltoft Museum – housed in three different buildings – the Old Town Hall, the Dyer's House and the Vicarage of Helgenæs. Check with the tourist office for times of opening. Glass Museum (*Glasmuseet*). Open daily, Mar–Dec. Doll Museum☆ with over 5,000 dolls. Open in summer.

36 Grenå Seaside town with ferry harbour. Djursland Museum has an interesting range of exhibits. Open daily, except Mons. Kattegatcentret☆ aquarium. Open daily.

37 Rosenholm Castle, Hornslet Renaissance building dating back to 1559. Richly decorated interior including 300 year old tapestries. Beautiful gardens. Open end Apr–early Aug.

38 Nimtofte Djurs Sommerland.☆ Well laid out activity park with over 50 attractions. Between Randers and Grenå. Open daily, mid-May – end Aug.

39 Gammel Estrup, Auning Renaissance castle founded c 1500 and rebuilt in the 17th century. Now a manor house and agricultural museum. Open daily, manor house closed Mons in winter.

40 Clausholm Castle, Voldum A five-winged mansion built in simple baroque style in 1699 – 1723. Chapel with Denmark's oldest organ. Extensive grounds with terraces and fountains. Open daily mid-June – end Aug.

41 Tange Elmuseet – illustrates the history of power production, distribution and consumption. Open daily, Apr– Oct.

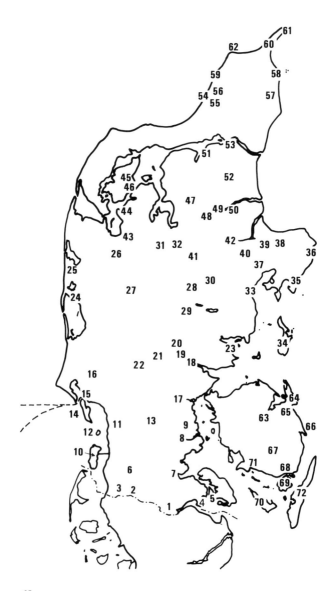

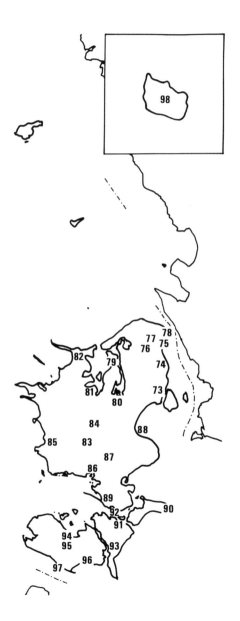

ATTRACTIONS FOR CHILDREN
AND ADULTS

42 Randers A commercial town on the river Gudenå. *Kulturhistorisk Museum* includes interiors from 1550 to the present day. Open Tues–Sun all year. Randers Art Museum (*Randers Kunstmuseum*) has Danish and foreign works of art from 1800 to the present day. Open Tues–Sun all year.

43 Hjerl Hede, Vinderup (near Skive) ☆ 2,500 acres of National Trust land by Lake Flynderrsø, part of which is devoted to a large scale open air museum. Many kinds of buildings, stone age settlement and forestry and peat digging museums. Surroundings are heather clad hills and forests of oak and pine. Open daily, Apr–Oct.

44 Spøttrup Castle, Balling (nearest town Skive) One of Denmark's finest medieval castles. Double moats, Herb Garden. Open daily, 1 May–23 Oct.

45 Nykøbing Mors *Støberimuseet* which features a large collection of stoves, kitchen ranges and cast iron ware. Open daily 22 June – 16 Aug. Morslands Historiske Museum tells the story of Mors and its people. Open daily.

46 Jesperhus Flower Park, Mors (near Nykøbing). Scandinavia's largest flower gardens with 500,000 plants. Also an aquarium and attractions for children.☆ Open daily May–Sept.

47 Ålestrup Bicycle museum☆ with about 100 bicycles and some early sewing machines and radios. Open daily. 1 May–31 Oct, except Mons.

48 Klejtrup Sø (lake), near Hobro ☆ Map of the world (scale 10.6 ins equals 68.9 miles) partly dug out of the shore and partly built out into the lake. Open May–Sept.

49 Fyrkat, near Hobro Remains of ring fortifications from the Viking Age c. 1000. Reconstructed Viking house. Open daily, Apr–Oct.

50 Mariager-Handest Veteran Railway ☆ Interesting collection of locomotives and rolling stock from Danish private railways. Runs Suns, June–Aug. Mariager is also a charming little town.

51 Nibe Best preserved little town of its period in the area of the Limfjord. Old buildings, narrow streets. Founded on herring fishing, now a quiet backwater.

52 Rebild Hills Splendid hilly area with the nearby *Rold Skov*, the largest forest in Denmark. The Rebild Hills (*Rebild Bakker*) form a national park donated by Danish-Americans in 1912. Lincoln log cabin includes an emigrants' museum and nearby is a museum of local history and folk music. At Thingbæk are former limestone mines which now house more than 100 works by the noted Danish sculptors Anders Bundgård and C.J. Bonnesen.

53 Ålborg large commercial city on the Limfjord. St. Budolfi Cathedral built in the Middle Ages. Large altar piece, carved pulpit and carillon of 48 bells. Holy Ghost Monastery (*Helligåndsklostret*). Cloisters from 1431 with interesting historical collection. Impressive merchants' houses: Jens Bang's House (1624) the largest Renaissance building in Scandinavia; and Jørgen Olufsen's House (1616). Interesting restored townscape with old buildings. Ålborg Historical Museum has a stone age collection. Open all year. North Jutland Museum of Art (*Nordjyllands Kunstmuseum*) has a unique collection of 20th century art. Open daily July–Aug, otherwise open daily except Mons. Ålborg Zoo. ☆ More than 1,500 animals. Open all year. Ålborg Tower, 344 ft above sea level. Magnificent views. Open daily, 1 Apr–3 Oct. Tivoliland. ☆ Large amusement park with 80 attractions and 15 restaurants. Open Apr–Sept. *Danmarks Tekniske Museum-Kommunikationsmuseet*. ☆ Inventions and developments in communications equipment. Open daily. *Søfarts & Marinemuseet*. ☆ The development of merchant and naval shipping in Denmark. Open daily 1 May–15 Sept (Wed, Sat, Sun spring and autumn). Lindholm Høje, near Ålborg. Biggest burial place in Scandinavia dating back to the iron age and Viking period. Open all year.

54 Blokhus-Løkken A broad stretch of sandy beach backed by sandhills. The sand is so firm that you can drive on it the entire distance from Blokhus to Løkken.

55 Fårup Sommerland, Saltum ☆ The pioneer Danish activity park. Includes a host of activities and has a huge Aqua park. Open early May-early Sept.

56 Børglum Monastery A massive and rather forbidding building. Episcopal residence 1150–1530. The garden, church, baptistry and recently restored Gothic organ are open to the public. Open 1 May–31 Aug.

57 Sæby Voergaard Castle. Renaissance building from 1586 with unique collection of art and porcelain. Open daily, end June–end Aug. Sct. Maria Klosterkirke. Abbey church built in Gothic style in 1469.

58 Frederikshavn International ferry port. The Gun Tower (*Krudttårnsmuseet*) built 1686–90 as part of the fortifications is now a museum of weapons and uniforms. Open daily, Apr–Oct. Bangsbo Museum (on the outskirts of the town) is a fascinating and well-arranged museum relating to Frederikshavn and district and housed in a manor house and farm buildings. Among subjects covered are shipping and the World War 2 occupation of Denmark. Display of old horse-drawn carriages and farm implements, Viking ship. Open daily, Apr–Oct. Cloostårnet, a 196ft high tower offering spectacular views (lift). Open 1 May–30 Sept.

ATTRACTIONS FOR CHILDREN
AND ADULTS

59 Rubjerg Knude, near Lønstrup   Nature reserve with large sand drifts and steep cliffs rising 240ft from the sea. The lighthouse, now closed, is completely dwarfed by the sandhills and is a sand drift museum.

60 Rabjerg Mile   An impressive migrating sand dune 875 yards wide by 1¼ miles long. A touch of the Sahara in Denmark.

61 Skagen   Northernmost town in Jutland and a great favourite with Danish artists, because of the quality of the light. The Skagen Museum contains many works from the golden age of Danish painting. Open daily, May–Sept (daily except Mons, Apr and Oct and for a more limited period during the rest of the year). Michael and Anna Anchers Hus – a well preserved artists' home with many of their paintings. Open daily, Apr–Oct (Otherwise Sat and Sun only). Open air musuem (*Skagen Fortidsminder*) includes old houses, windmill and a fisheries museum. Beyond Skagen is Grenen, at the very tip of Jutland where the waters of the Kattegat meet the Skagerrak. You can walk over the sandhills to the point and ride a tractor train.

62 Hirtshals   Nordsømuseet – a salt water aquarium with fish from the North Sea plus a sealarium. Museum of Danish fishing and fishing research. Open daily.

FUNEN

63 Odense   Third largest city in Denmark and birthplace of Hans Christian Andersen. The H.C. Andersen Museum☆ tells the story of his life and includes many of his personal belongings. Open all year. His childhood home forms another museum. Open all year. Danish State Railway Museum☆. Locomotives, coaches, models and relics from Denmark's railways of the past. Open daily mid-Apr – end Sept, Sundays Oct–Apr. Funen village (*Den Fynske Landsby*).☆ An open air museum with old houses, farms, schools, mill, etc. Open daily, Apr–Mid-Oct (rest of the year Suns only). Fyns Tivoli.☆ Funfair with rides, etc. Open Apr–Aug. St. Canutes Cathedral (*Sct Knudskirke*), Denmark's most significant Gothic church building. Brandts Klaedefabrik, cultural centre with changing visual and decorative art and architectural exhibitions. Also houses the Museum of Photographic Art (*Museet for Fotokunst*) and Danish Museum of Printing (*Danmarks Grafiske Museum*). Open daily, except Mons. Møntergården – museum of urban history with a fascinating range of exhibits. Open daily. Museum of the life and work of composer Carl Nielsen. Hollufgård cultural centre which includes a museum of Funen and its inhabitants and a 70-acre prehistoric environment. Open daily, except Mons, 1 May – 15 Oct. European Car Museum☆ (near Odense). 70 cars on display. Open daily July–Aug and at weekends spring and autumn.

64 Kerteminde Johannes Larsen Museet – museum in the home of the Funen painter Johannes Larsen. Open daily, except Mons, Mar–Oct (open Wed and Sun Nov–Feb). Museum in a merchant's house from 1630 with a wide range of interesting exhibits. Open daily, 1 Mar–31 Oct.

65 Ladby Viking Ship (*Ladby skibet*), near Kerteminde This Viking ship, c.900, was a chief's grave. Open daily, except Mons.

66 Nyborg Denmark's oldest and only example of a royal castle from the medieval period. Interiors from the Middle Ages and weapon collection. Open daily June–Aug (closed Mons Mar–May).

67 Egeskov Castle, Kværndrup One of the loveliest Renaissance castles to be found anywhere in Europe. Built 1524–54. Beautiful park with a labyrinth. Veteran transport museum☆ with cars and aircraft. Open daily, 1 May–30 Sept.

68 Svendborg The oldest house in this pleasant town, Anne Hvides Gård (1560), is now part of the Svendborg and district museum. Sct. Nicolaj Church built c. 1200 in Romanesque style. Toy Museum (*Legetøjsmuseet*)☆ includes changing exhibitions. Open daily, 1 June – 31 Aug (1–31 May and 1 Sept – 31 Dec daily except Mon, Tues). Veteran ship '*Helge*' makes sightseeing trips from 6 June – 14 Aug.

69 Tåsinge A charming island facing Svendborg across the Sound and linked by a bridge. The pretty village of Troense has a fascinating shipping museum (*Søfartssamlingen*). Open daily (not Suns Nov–Apr). Valdemars Castle, built 1639–43, is now a manor house museum with impressive interiors and art collection. Open daily, May–Sept (open Sat, Sun in Apr and Oct). Has beautiful location.

70 Ærø One of the most beautiful islands in Denmark and reached by ferry from Svendborg, Fåborg, Rudkøbing or Mommark. The principal town – Ærøskøbing – is *the* fairytale town with its old-world atmosphere and narrow cobbled streets with little houses. Ærø Museum, regional museum in a 1755 house. Open daily, mid-May – mid–Sept. Hammerich's House with faience, furniture and tiles. Open June–Aug. Ships in bottles museum. Open daily. At Marstal, the other town on the island, is the Maritime Museum (*Marstal Søfartsmuseum*) has many interesting artefacts and over 40 ship models. Open daily. Marstal Church (1737) has six ship models hanging in the nave and the altar piece is unusual as the faces of the apostles are those of local skippers, long deceased.

71 Fåborg Museum of Funen Painting. Open daily. Kaleko Mølle – a restored 600 year old mill, now a museum. Fåborg

Kulturhistoriske Museum is in an 18th century merchant's house and the exhibits are displayed in 21 rooms. Open daily, mid-May – mid-Sept.

72 Langeland Long, thin island (32 miles by 7 miles) reached by bridge from Tåsinge. At Tranekær is the imposing red-painted Tranekær Castle beside the Borresø lake (park open to the public). Rudkøbing, the principal town, has many old houses. Aquarium Langeland. ☆ Open daily.
Herrgården Skovsgaard, south of Rudkøbing, is a manor house now housing the Forestry Museum (*Skovbrugsmuseum*) and Carriage Museum (*Vognmuseum*). Open Suns, May–Sept.

ZEALAND

73 Copenhagen See separate chapter on Denmark's capital on page 132.

74 Rungsted Karen Blixen Museum which is devoted to this unorthodox and controversial figure, perhaps best known in the UK as the authoress of the original book from which the film '*Out of Africa*' was adapted. The museum is in the house where she was born and where she died. Open daily May–Sept (Oct–Apr daily except Tues).

75 Humlebæk Louisiana, a most impressive and beautifully sited museum of modern art and cultural centre on the coast between Copenhagen and Helsingør. Extensive permanent collection plus regular exhibitions. Open daily.

76 Hillerød Frederiksborg Castle – built 1600–21 and now housing the National Historical Museum which makes a fine setting for the furniture, paintings and portraits illustrating Denmark's past. About 70 rooms can be seen including the Knight's Hall, the Audience Chamber and the Chapel. The latter has a Compenius organ from 1610. Open all year. N.Zealand Folk Museum (*Nordsjællandsk Folkemuseum*) has varied collection ranging from costumes to toys. Open mid-June–Sept, not Mons, otherwise open Suns only.

77 Fredensborg Fredensborg Palace – built in the early 18th century in Italian style. A residence of the Danish Royal Family. Part of the palace is open in July, while the extensive park is open all year.

78 Helsingør Kronborg Castle, an impressive building which was the setting for Shakespeare's 'Hamlet'. Magnificent Great Hall while the King's and Queen's apartments are most noteworthy. The Chapel still looks as it was in 1582. There is a separate Mercantile and Maritime Museum (*Handels og Søfartsmuseet*) with 27 rooms and many beautiful ship models. Open daily, closed Mons Mar–Oct. Denmark's Technical Museum. ☆ History of natural science and technology with 2,000 items for everyday use. Separate Traffic Museum with a good selection of cars, motor cycles, bicycles and model railways. Open daily. Helsingør Town Museum (*Helsingør Bymuseum*).☆ Housed in the old 16th century Carmelite friary. Of particular interest is a detailed model of the town in the year 1801. Also many dolls. Open daily.

79 Jægerspris Castle, dating back to the Middle Ages and acquired by King Frederik VII in 1854. The king's apartments are open to the public and are exactly as when the monarch died in 1863. Open daily, except Mons 1 May–30 Sept. Guided tours only.

80 Roskilde Impressive 12th century cathedral, the Danish equivalent of Westminster Abbey. Some 38 kings and queens are entombed in the cathedral in elaborate and varied sarcophagi. Viking ship Museum (*Vikingskibshallen*).☆ Houses five 11th century Viking ships which were recovered from the Roskilde Fjord. Also other material relating to Viking ships, etc. Open daily. Lützhøfts Købmandsgård.☆ A merchant's house restored as a general store in the 1910–20 period. More than 100 items of the period offered for sale. Open daily, 1 June–31 Aug (otherwise daily except Suns). Roskilde Museum and the Museum of Roskilde Cathedral (opening 1993) are other places of interest. At the Lejre Research Centre (*Lejre Forsøgscenter*) near Roskilde is an experimental reconstruction of an Iron Age settlement☆ with buildings, workshops, tools and so on. Open daily, 1 May–28 Sept.

81 Holbæk The Museum of Holbæk and District (*Museet for Holbæk og Omegn*) is a fascinating museum housed in nine old buildings which illustrate the development of Holbæk and the surrounding area. Open all year, closed Mons.

82 Nykøbing Sj. Sjælland Sommerland.☆ Activity park with over 60 attractions. Open daily 20 May–29 Aug. Nykøbing's museum includes an old bakery, grocer's shop, the town history and a kitchen garden. Open daily Apr–Oct, otherwise Mon–Fri.

83 Ringsted Fantasy World.☆ Hundreds of mechanical figures in their own fairytale world. Open daily (closed Mons 19 Apr–24 May. Also closed 1 Mar–2 Apr and 20 Sept–8 Oct). Ringsted Landbrugsmuseum covers the cultural history of central Zealand. Open daily, not Sats.

84 Skjoldenæsholm, Jystrup Tram Museum☆ with operating vintage trams from former Danish tramways. Open May–Oct, weekends (also Tues, Wed, Thur in peak summer).

85 Trelleborg, near Slagelse Impressive fortified Viking camp, partly reconstructed. Open daily, 11 Apr–13 Sept.

ATTRACTIONS FOR CHILDREN
AND ADULTS

86 Næstved Gavnø Manor. A Rococo palace (1755–58). Interiors and art collection. Chapel. Open daily, May–Aug. Sparresholm Carriage Collection, near Næstved, has a collection of carriages and horse-drawn vehicles. Open Sats and Suns, 12 May–7 Aug. Also near Næstved is the Holmegård Glassworks at Fensmark. Open Mon–Fri and also Sats, Suns from early Apr to mid-Oct. (Note: closed for three weeks in July).

87 Gisselfeld Abbey, near Haslev Built in 1554 and later twice rebuilt. Set in one of Denmark's most beautiful parks, laid out in English style and extending to over 100 acres. Open daily, late March-end Aug.

88 Køge 700-year old market town with many fine well-preserved half-timbered houses. A half hour's drive away are the cliffs of Stevns Klint. Museum.

89 Vordingborg Old market town with remains of 12th century castle. The Goose Tower (*Gåsetårnet*), Denmark's best preserved medieval tower. Open daily, mid-May – mid-Sept.

MØN

90 Møns Klint Fascinating chalk formations on the east coast of the island of Møn. They stretch for eight miles and rise to a height of 420ft above sea level. The highest point is the Queen's Chair (*Dronningstolen*). Liselund, a short drive from the cliffs, has a romantic little Empire-style thatched chateau, called the Danish 'Petit Trianon' and built in 1795. Set in a beautiful park in which are three 18th century summerhouses: the Chinese House, the Norwegian House and the Swiss Cottage.

FALSTER

91 Stubbekøbing Motorcycle and Radio Museum.☆ Over 120 motorcycles from 1897 onwards. Also vintage radios and gramophones. Open daily, 1 June-31 Aug (weekends in May and Sept).

92 Farø Linking the island of Sjælland and Falster are two impressive bridges which straddle the tiny island of Farø on which is the Danish Highway Museum (*Danmarks Vejmuseum*). Illustrates the history of Danish roads and highways. Open daily.

93 Nykøbing Fl. 700-year old market town by the Guldborgsund. At Sundby is the Medieval Centre for Historical Technology (*Middlelaldecentre*)☆ where one can see how people in the middle ages worked, played and even waged war. Open mid-May – mid–Sept daily, except Mons. Museum for the cultural history of Falster (*Museet Falstersminde*) illustrates the town's history and is housed in two 17th century buildings. Open daily, except Mons.

LOLLAND

94 Knuthenborg Safari Park ☆Between Maribo and Bandholm. Europe's biggest manorial park with 500 different species of trees and shrubs while the safari park has more than 900 animals. Open daily, May–late Sept.

95 Maribo-Bandholm Veteran Railway ☆Operates vintage trains on summer weekends.

96 Ålholm Castle, Nysted Much extended castle with one wing open to the public. The 62 acre park contains many different species of trees. Open daily, 1 June–end Aug. The Ålholm Automobile Museum☆ which lies to the west of the castle contains a fine collection of over 200 veteran and vintage cars. A train in the style of the 1850's links the museum with the seaside. Open daily, 1 June–1 Sept.

97 Lalandia ☆Denmark's largest sub-tropical swimscape situated on the southern tip of Lolland near Rødby Havn. Open daily.

98 Bornholm See separate chapter on this beautiful Baltic island on page 135.

Note: General literature issued by the Danish Tourist Board and brochures published by the various regional tourist offices provide additional information on places of interest and current times of opening.

SPORTS AND RECREATIONS

Swimming and bathing With 4,500 miles of coastline Denmark provides plenty of opportunities for swimming and bathing. There are miles of fine beaches, many of which are entitled to fly the EC's Blue Flag, and they are frequently backed by sandhills. The west coast of Jutland has the longest stretches of sandy beach, but of course it faces the North Sea where you are more than likely to encounter windy conditions.

A more placid environment will be found on the east Jutland coast and around the islands of Funen and Zealand. There are quite a few good beaches which shelve gently into the water which makes them very safe for children. On the island of Bornholm you will find both a rocky coastline and areas with beautiful fine white sand.

All beaches are open freely to the public and none has been 'developed' as in so many other countries. At only a few places is bathing not allowed and this is usually around harbours. Nude bathing is permitted on many parts of the coast and topless bathing and sunbathing is commonplace.

If sea bathing does not appeal then you will find plenty of excellent public swimming pools while many hotels and holiday centres have indoor or outdoor pools. There are the popular aqua parks where you can bathe with added thrills.

Fishing With its extensive coastline, and plenty of well-stocked rivers and lakes, Denmark is a splendid country for the angler but fishing permits are compulsory for all kinds of fishing. Licences are obtainable from post offices (Dkr 25 for a week or Dkr 75 for a month). For sea fishing there are numerous harbours where you can go out with an experienced local boatman and enjoy some really good sport. Off-shore fishing is allowed from virtually all stretches of the shore accessible to the public. Check with the local tourist office for information on the best places to go.

Freshwater fishing is very good and Denmark has an excellent reputation with British anglers. Rivers in Jutland are probably the best. Check with the local tourist office who can provide information as fishing rights in lakes and rivers are usually privately owned. They can also provide details of local angling opportunities. Addresses of Danish angling societies can be obtained from *Danmarks Sportsfiskerforbund, Worsaaesgade 1, DK-7100 Vejle*.

Sailing Danish waters are ideal for sailing and there are something like 500 harbours plus many well-equipped marinas. There are both open and sheltered waters and there are few places around the country where you cannot enjoy sailing. The area around south Funen and on the Limfjord are both sheltered and very attractive.

Boats of all kinds can be hired, but rates are generally higher than in the UK.

On a smaller scale, there are opportunities for canoeing on several rivers, the best one being the Gudenå in Jutland. Again it is possible to hire canoes.

Golf This has become an increasingly popular leisure pursuit in Denmark. From having only a handful of golf courses 20 years ago, there are now over 70 courses, about half of which are 18-hole. Visiting golfers are welcome and all you need is your club membership card. Green fees are modest: weekdays Dkr 80–120, weekends and bank holidays Dkr 200–250. Details of golf courses, opening times, etc., are available from *Dansk Golf Union, Toftevej 26, DK-2625 Vallensbæk*.

Riding The number of horses and ponies in Denmark has increased at a surprising rate over the last few years. Consequently there are plenty of opportunities to ride and there is also plenty of enjoyable riding country. There are many riding schools with animals suitable for beginners or experts and for children or adults. Charges are broadly the same as those in Britain.

There are some riding holidays available and also riding camps for young people on Jutland and Funen. You can also hire a horse-drawn prairie wagon on Funen, Langeland and Samsø.

Cycling Denmark is an ideal cycling country with its undulating scenery and no severe gradients. There are something like 28,600 miles of minor roads mainly carrying only local traffic which are very suitable for the cyclist while there are many miles of cycle paths. Inclusive cycling holidays are available and you can also rent a bike – useful if you want to give up the car for a day or two and do some healthy pedalling.

Various There are many other activities which can involve the visitor. Here are just a few: archaeology, botany, bird-watching, ceramics, dyeing, drawing, lace-making, painting, tennis, walking, weaving and windsurfing.

Meet the Danes In Århus and Odense there is a scheme in operation that lets you meet a local Danish family. You visit them in their home and have an opportunity to learn more about everyday life in Denmark. Contact the tourist office.

THE ITINERARIES – AN INTRODUCTION

ALL THE ROUTES in the itineraries have been personally checked, with one or two minor exceptions. In certain instances I have given what might be called a simplified route when suggesting minor roads. An examination of a good map will show that more complex – and perhaps more interesting – routes can be followed if you have the time (and the ability to read a map).

I have suggested overnight stops and have also recommended those centres where you should stay more than one night so you can do some additional sightseeing. These extra nights can be eliminated if you cannot spare the time.

In the chapter 'Attractions for Children and Adults' the various entries are numbered and where these are also referred to in the itineraries, they are cross-referenced with the same number. You should refer to these entries as this information is not necessarily repeated in the itineraries. In the same way, any attractions for children are indicated with a ☆.

Those hotels, inns or restaurants which I have visited will often merit rather more description than those which are merely listed for general information purposes. The listed ones may be perfectly satisfactory, but it is simply a case of having no personal knowledge of them.

I would also issue the same word of caution that I have expressed elsewhere that many attractions, museums and so on are only open in summer or may have very limited opening hours for the rest of the year. If you are motoring around Denmark in the autumn or spring you may have to suffer a more restricted cultural diet, but this should not discourage you from going to Denmark outside the summer season. The scenery and the food and drink are just as good and there is even less traffic on the roads while tour operators may have some very good value packages available.

You will see that I have not included detailed mileages between overnight centres and instead I have given a mileage guide. This is quite deliberate because of the difficulty of determining exact mileages where the smaller roads are involved. Even the Danish kilometre distances on signposts do not always speak the truth! Finally, make sure that you have the right maps.

Although the itineraries are virtually unchanged to those in previous editions of *Drive around Denmark* they have been completely updated and some additional ones are included.

Nearly all the itineraries begin at Esbjerg because of its direct ferry connection to the UK. If you motor to Denmark via Germany and cross the border at either Padborg or Tønder it is quite simple to join any of the itineraries at a suitable point.

If you decide to fly and rent a car then your best option is to use the Maersk Air service to Billund as you are then only 36 miles from Esbjerg.

Continued on page 81

Denmark's little Sahara - and not a camel in sight. Rabjerg Mile is a migrating dune near the northern tip of Jutland. It stretches for over a mile.

73

ABOVE - In various parts of Denmark are activity parks called
'Sommerlands'. This is Fårup Sommerland in northern Jutland
showing part of the Aqua Park.

BELOW - Danish town centres in summer are places to meet and
chat or do nothing. This scene is at Nykøbing F1. on the island
of Falster.

74

ABOVE - Denmark's best known culinary achievement is the open sandwich (Smørrebrød). The most minor part is the piece of bread - what goes on top can be almost anything. An ice cold aquavit (in the small glass) and a beer go down well with your Smørrebrød.

BELOW – A Danish inn is a kro and many of them are old and attractive. This is the Sønderho Kro on the island of Fanø.

Denmark's scenery is tranquil and very easy on the eye but never (with one or two exceptions) is it boring. This is a typical landscape near Holbæk on Zealand.

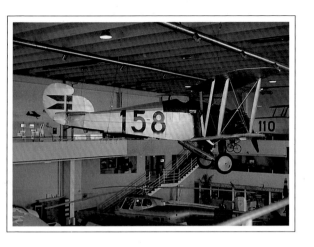

ABOVE - One of the newer attractions is the Center Mobilium, a superb modern museum of aircraft, cars and salvage and rescue vehicles. This is just one corner of the aircraft section.

BELOW – Inside the Eksperimentarium at Hellerup, Copenhagen. This is a 'hands on' science centre which appeals to both children and adults.

The elaborate banqueting hall at Frederiksborg Castle at Hillerød on Zealand. It houses the National Historical Museum and is a fine setting for furniture, paintings and portraits illustrating Denmark's past.

ABOVE - The little harbour at Gudhjem on the beautiful Baltic island of Bornholm. Coming into the harbour is the boat from the tiny island of Christiansø.

BELOW - Liseland, the romantic little Empire-style thatched chateau, often called the Danish 'Petit Trianon'. It is on the island of Møn and nearby are impressive 400ft high chalk cliffs known as Møns Klint.

In the Railway Museum in Odense there are plenty of full-size historical railway exhibits. No.45, seen here, was built in 1869 by Robert Stephenson & Co., at Newcastle-upon-Tyne.

SOUTH JUTLAND, FUNEN AND A SPRINKLING OF THE ISLANDS

THIS ITINERARY takes you across Jutland, via Legoland (for those with children) to Vejle, on the attractive Vejle Fjord. Here you should stay two nights to allow for my suggested excursions. You continue south, across the Little Belt bridge to Funen and then take a roundabout route via Bogense to Odense. As there is plenty to see here, a two night stay is recommended. Svendborg, in the south of the island is your next objective, calling at Egeskov Castle en route.

At Svendborg you can make excursions to the islands of Tåsinge and Langeland which are linked by bridges, and to the beautiful island of Ærø, which is reached by ferry.

Your journey continues through the delightful Funen countryside and back on to the peninsula of Jutland to Kolding. You now head south through Christiansfeld, Haderslev (night stop) and Åbenrå to Sønderborg which is a bridge span away on the island of Als. Then westward to Tønder, a picturesque little town and, after an overnight stop, on to Møgeltønder and on to the island of Rømø which is linked to Jutland by a long causeway. Ribe is your last night stop before motoring to Esbjerg.

Ideally you need 10 nights in Denmark, but this can be reduced to eight if necessary. Alternatively for a shorter stay you can either concentrate on Funen and the islands or, on south Jutland.

DAY 1

Leave Esbjerg on the E20 towards Kolding and after about seven miles take the left fork marked to Grindsted (road 30). Bypass the town and follow the signs to Billund (road 28). This town is the home of Denmark's best known toy – Lego. It is also the home of Denmark's second biggest attraction. Legoland ☆ (**21**). If you have children with you a stop at Legoland is essential; the problem will be getting them away from it. But grown-ups will also find it fascinating with its many different attractions, both indoors and outdoors (it also has good restaurants and a cafeteria). Billund has another attraction: the superb Mobilium☆ a combination of three museums – cars, aircraft and rescue and salvage vehicles. Worth a visit. Continue on road 28 to Vejle.

Vejle (**18**) enjoys a notable position at the end of the beautiful Vejle Fjord. Since they built the motorway, which bypasses the town (and crosses the fjord on an immense bridge) the centre has become much improved, especially in summer. Places of interest: Gothic-style Sct. Nicolai Church which has inside it the preserved body of a 2,500-year-old woman found in the Haraldskær Bog; art and town museums; and the town's landmark a windmill.

High hills rise on both sides of the fjord providing good views. Big park on the north side of the fjord, while the road on the south side leads to Munkebjerg (321 ft above sea level), a very beautiful area of woods and walks, in the centre of which is the

SOUTH JUTLAND, FUNEN AND A
SPRINKLING OF THE ISLANDS

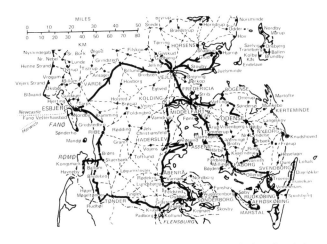

Munkebjerg Hotel. I consider this to be one of the best hotels in Denmark – for location, comfort and food. It has a splendid position, an excellent restaurant, bar, casino, indoor pool, sauna and solarium and billiards and tennis courts. Vejle golf course is nearby. Other hotels in Vejle include the Scandic Australia, the modern and comfortable Vejle Center, Park, Dann Inn and Motel Hedegården (nearby). Youth hostel. Camping site.

DAY 2

Suggested excursions for Vejle. Leave the town on the old main road north (170) and on the outskirts turn right on road 23, which passes through a mix of scenery to Juelsminde, a minor holiday town. Take the coast road (459) north to Glud, where you bear right to the quiet little fishing hamlet of Snaptun. Minor ferry connection to Hjarnø. There is a much enlarged and modernised inn, the Snaptun Færgegård. Return to Glud where there is an interesting museum of Danish rural life. (**23**). Worth a visit.

Continue along the same road towards Horsens, with the Horsens Fjord in the distance on the right. Beyond the little village of Sejet take a minor road on the left to Bjerre. This takes you through the rather pleasant Bjerre Skov (forest) with attractive walks (plenty of parking places). Follow signs to Sønder (turn right) and then turn left at Nørre Bjerre. This takes you via Stenderup to road 170 where you turn left and return to Vejle, entering the town on the same road from which you departed.

The second excursion takes you out of Vejle to the north west on the Grejsdalsvej which leads you through the pretty Grejs valley with its densely wooded hillsides and varied landscape. At Sandvad turn left on a minor road which leads you to road 18. If you have children, turn right to visit the Safari Park ☆ (**20**), near Givskud. Alternatively, turn left to Jelling (**19**) to see the ancient burial mounds and runic stones in the Churchyard. You can also take a veteran steam train from Vejle to Jelling on Sundays in July and early August. From here it is only 7½ miles back to Vejle. Another excursion, without your car, is to take a motor boat trip on the fjord (about 1½ hours, check times with the tourist office).

DAY 3

Leave Vejle on the E133 south. It joins the E20 near the Little Belt which you cross via the imposing suspension bridge. Once across the bridge, on Funen, take the exit off the motorway and then turn left, crossing over the E20 and follow signs to Bogense. This is something of a quiet backwater, made up of gently rolling farmland. *Bogense* is a little town with a small harbour, a marina and some quiet streets. Hotels: Bogense Hotel, Bogense Kyst Hotel. Camping site close to the beach.

Take the Søndersø road (311) and in the village turn right to Morud (road 335), turn left and shortly afterwards take a little road to the right which takes you through wooded countryside and past Langesø manor house (not open to the public). You come back to the Morud road (turn left), then to the E20 (join it in the Odense direction). Follow signs into *Odense* (**63**).

DAY 4

With its various places of interest (the principal ones linked with its most famous son, Hans Christian Andersen) it deserves a two night stay. Although an important commercial city, and even having a major shipyard, you do not really notice the industry. Hotels: H.C. Andersen and Odense Plaza (both large, modern), Windsor (in dull surroundings, but comfortable), Grand (large), City Hotel Odense, Missionshotellet Ansgar, Motel Odense (off-centre, on ring road) and Scandic Hotel Odense (5 miles from city centre). Two camping sites. Youth hostel. Boat trips on the Odense river (see **63** for other attractions).

DAY 5

Leave Odense on road 9 to Kværndrup, then right on road 8, and soon afterwards watch for the right turn to Egeskov Castle ☆ (**67**). A visit to see this fine building and the beautiful park should not be missed. The transport and carriage museums are additional attractions. Return to road 8 and turn right towards Fåborg. This will take you past, on the left, the imposing collection of buildings that make up Brahetrolleborg, the oldest of which was a 15th century abbey. Park open to the public. Restaurant by the park entrance. Just beyond is the village of Korinth (Korinth Kro on the right). Left on road 43 for the final run in to Fåborg.

Fåborg (**71**) has some picturesque features including Vesterport, the town gate (one of the few to be preserved) and the bell tower, the remains of Sct. Nikolaj church, Fåborg's interesting museum is in an 18th c. merchant's house. Art museum with Funen paintings. Pleasant pedestrian precinct. Leave on road 44 towards Svendborg, but on the outskirts you can fork left on a minor road to Kaleko where there is a restored 600-year-old mill which is now a museum. On the outskirts is the Holiday Hotel Klinten (large, self-catering) and the Hotel Fåborg Fjord.

Although it is a modest commercial centre *Svendborg* (**68**) is also a superb base for the holidaymaker as the southern part of Funen and its off-shore islands are so delightful. It enjoys the almost perfect location by the Sound which is protected by the islands of Thurø and Tåsinge. You really need to spend three nights here, although this could be reduced to two. Hotels: Hotel Svendborg (central, good restaurant, pleasant bedrooms), Ærø, Hotel Royal, Tre Roser (on the outskirts and both a hotel and self-catering centre).

Just outside the town is Christiansminde, a delightful park and beach. Youth hostel which enjoys a nice location. Beyond the park turn right over the causeway on to the horseshoe-shaped little island of *Thurø*. Rather pretty, with two well placed camping sites.

DAYS 6 AND 7

Suggested excursions from Svendborg. One day must be earmarked for a visit to the idyllic island of *Ærø* (**70**). The ferry takes 70 minutes and on a sunny day there is no better way of passing the time.

Ærøskøbing, where you disembark, is a gem and deserves to be wandered round and savoured. *Marstal*, the old skipper town, is not so pretty-pretty but should also be visited, while the drive from one to the other is very enjoyable. Approaching the town the road runs alongside the beach (mainly shingle) where there are good parking places. There is one main road along the length of the island, running through a series of villages, to another small ferry port, Søby (connections to Fåborg and Mommark).

There is a limited number of hotels on the island, the principal ones being Ærøskøbing – Ærøhus, Det Lille Hotel and Marina (new, with self-catering facilities); Marstal – Ærø Strand, and Marstal. Camping sites at Ærøskøbing, Marstal and Søby. Youth hostel at Marstal.

For another day out, cross the bridge from Svendborg to the picturesque island of *Tåsinge* (**69**). Follow the signs to *Troense*, which is deservedly called one of the best preserved villages in Denmark. Make a point of seeing the fascinating little maritime museum (*Søfartssamlingen*). Overlooking the Sound, and with splendid views, is the Hotel Troense which has motel-style rooms at the rear. Nearby is Valdemars Castle which enjoys a beautiful setting and includes an impressive museum of interiors. Restaurant in the vaults and a bistro called the Applegarden. As an alternative to driving you can, in mid-summer, sail in the little veteran ship '*Helge*' from Svendborg.

If you want to see the island from another viewpoint climb the tower of Bregninge Church. Across the road from the church is a small, but interesting, folklore museum and sea captain's house. At Landet Church you can see the result of a Mayerling-like tragedy. In 1899 Count Sparre killed his lover, the circus artist Elvira Madigan, and then shot himself. Both of them are buried in the churchyard.

Continue across the island and over the causeway and bridge to the island of *Langeland* (72). *Rudkøbing*, the 'capital', is an attractive little town with some well preserved old houses. Museum. Hotel Rudkøbing and Rudkøbing Skudehavn. Youth hostel. Take the road via Simmerbølle and Tullebølle to *Tranekær* which goes through rolling well-wooded countryside. This pleasant village has, at one end, the impressive red-painted bulk of Tranekær Castle beside the Borresø (lake). There is access to the park. Cafeteria in the former stables or you can refresh yourself at the Tranekær Gjæstgivergaard (inn) near the castle. Lohals at the northern end of the island is a little dull, while at the other end is Bagenkop, a small fishing town which tends to be overrun with holidaymakers from Germany. Nearby is a range of cliffs and a good beach at Ristinge.

If you have time you can also visit, by ferry, the other smaller islands off the coast of Funen, which are *Skarø, Drejø* and *Strynø*.

DAY 8

Leave Svendborg on road 44 to Fåborg, following the signs to Hårby. Beyond Millinge you will see on the right, the drive leading to Steensgaard Herregårdspension. This impressive three-winged manor house (*c.* 1535) is now an hotel and offers a unique atmosphere with its period style bedrooms (but with modern bathrooms) and beautifully furnished sitting rooms and attractive restaurant. The 27-acre park provides peaceful surroundings and it is the sort of place to which I should certainly like to return.

A little further along the road, on the left, is the Faldsled Kro which is renowned for its cuisine (and has prices to match its reputation). At Hårby you take the road (329) to Glamsbjerg. Watch for a right turn to Ørsted and go through the village and then follow the sign to Tommerup. On the left is Frøbjerg Bavnehøj, the highest point on Funen (346 ft above sea level). It is an easy climb to the summit where you can enjoy some good views of this part of the island. Return to Ørsted and the main road (turn left) to Assens. Before reaching the latter, turn right on road 313 to Middelfart via Hjorte and Udby. This is an easygoing secondary road that cuts across rural countryside which is now, as in other areas, largely devoted to cereal crops.

On the approach to Middelfart you join the old main road (161) linking Odense with Jutland and which crosses the Little Belt by the first bridge which was completed in 1935. On the approach to the bridge there is a parking area and cafeteria and you can also take a small road on the left which leads down to Hindsgaul, a manor house built in 1785 and now a conference centre and hotel. From here you can walk through the woods to the seashore. You will see a sign to Mindelunden which is a memorial grove dedicated to British aircrew shot down in World War 2. There is a good camping site on this attractive peninsula.

After crossing the Little Belt you keep to the old main road (161) which provides good views of Kolding Fjord on the left. At Taulov, on the right, is the very attractive Kryb-i-Ly inn with some English touches to the furnishings. Follow signs into *Kolding* (**17**) with its massive castle, part of which is a museum. Not the easiest town to drive around, there is a good car park on the left opposite the lake and reasonably close to the castle. Hotels: Saxildhus (by the station), Kolding (near the castle), Hotel Tre Roser and Scanticon-Kolding (hotel and conference centre), Scandic Hotel and Hotel Koldingfjord on the outskirts and facing the fjord. The latter is near the Kunstmuseet Trapholt a splendid 20th c. art museum. Camping sites. Youth hostel.

Depart on the Haderslev road (170), making sure you avoid the E45 motorway. Leave the main road where it is signed to *Christiansfeld* (**9**), the unusual little town established in 1773 by the Moravian Brethren. Two museums: one devoted to the Community of Brethren while the other is the South Jutland Fire Brigade Museum – a strange contrast. The church can hold 1,000 worshippers. The town's speciality (apart from its architecture) is its honey cake.

Continue south on road 170 to *Haderslev* (**8**) which has an interesting and historic centre and an impressive cathedral. There is a spacious park beside the Haderslev Dam (lake). Hotels: Golf Hotel Norden (in the park), Harmonien and Motel Haderslev. Camping site. Youth hostel. This makes a suitable overnight stop or you can go a little further south to Åbenrå. You can deviate on a secondary road from Christiansfeld which will take you to the Danish national monument at Skamlingsbanken (good views).

DAY 9

When you leave Haderslev divert on to the road to Osby and Årøsund (small ferry to the island of Årø). Return on the alternative road via Vilstrup, rejoining the main road near Hoptrup. This little excursion is in no way dramatic, just a nice change from motoring down the main road.

Åbenrå (**7**) is a rather disappointing town; it has some nice old streets, but it has been somewhat overwhelmed by commercial development. At the end of the wide Åbenrå Fjord it should enjoy splendid views but these are spoiled by oil storage tanks on one side and a monumental power station on the other. Interesting museum. Hotel Europa. Youth hostel. Numerous camping sites in the area.

Instead of taking the main road to Sønderborg, turn left shortly after passing the power station, and continue through some very enjoyable scenery with occasional views of the Als Fjord. You rejoin the main road a few miles from Sønderborg.

Sønderborg (5) on the island of Als, is linked by bridges to Jutland. Impressive castle, busy shopping centre and with attractive surroundings. Hotels: Ansgar, City, Garni, Strandpavillonen and Scandic. Return across the Sound taking the Kruså road (8). On the outskirts is Dybbøl Banke (4) with its cannon and ramparts associated with the Danish-German war of 1864.

Shortly afterwards take the right fork in the road (481) to *Gråsten*, where the royal summer palace is to be found. The park is open to the public except when the Royal Family is in residence. The palace is now a little overshadowed by industry.

Rejoin the main Kruså road but at Rinkenæs bear left on to the secondary road which runs alongside the Flensborg Fjord. This is a delightful drive through Rønshoved, Sønderhav and Kollund. Several hotels and restaurants along this stretch, plus two well-placed camping sites and a youth hostel.

At the main crossroads at Kruså continue straight ahead (turn left and you are almost immediately at the German frontier) on road 8 near Smedby, turn left on a minor road (over the Motorway), to Frøslev. This was an internment camp for Danes in World War 2 and is now a museum and memorial (1). Near Fårhus rejoin Road 8 to Tønder.

Tønder (2) is worth looking at, with its many preserved houses and an excellent museum. Hotels: Hostrups, Motel Apartments and Abild. Camping site. Youth hostel.

DAY 10

Take the Højer road (419) out of Tønder which brings you to the pretty little village of *Møgeltønder* (3). With its cobbled street lined with lime trees and little houses it is very picturesque, while the village church has the oldest working church organ in Denmark (1679). At one end of the village is the Schackenborg Palace and also the Schackenborg Kro.

You can make an intriguing little detour by taking the minor road on the left, beyond Møgeltønder, which is marked to Rudbøl. This is flat, marshland country with an atmosphere of its own. The farms are on raised mounds so that, in the past, they avoided flooding. *Rudbøl* is a most unusual village as the Danish-German border runs down the main street. Danish locals, for example, go shopping at the German supermarket and can be seen wheeling their trolleys back over the border to their cars. Just short of the border is the Rudbøl Grænsekro – an inn dating back to 1791. Behind the old building is a modern complex which is used as a conference centre. There are also some holiday cabins.

The food is to be recommended with several marshland specialities. This inn would make an alternative place to stay to Tønder. From Rudbøl take the Højer road and continue north via Vester Gammelby and then bear left to take the coast road (419) via Koldby and Badsbøl. Then take the left turn (road 175) to the island of *Rømø* (**10**) which is reached via a six mile long causeway.

When you reach the island, if you drive straight ahead you will come to the magnificent beach which stretches along the west coast. If you turn left this will take you down to the fishing port of Havneby (ferry to Sylt). The north west corner of the island is a restricted military zone. Out of season Rømø is a sleepy place but in high summer it attracts many tourists and is particularly popular with German holidaymakers.

Returning across the causeway, continue to the main road (11) and turn left to Ribe. When you approach the town leave the ring road and follow signs to the centre. *Ribe* (**11**) is my favourite small town in south Jutland. With its dominant and impressive cathedral in the centre, and the many beautifully preserved houses in the little streets, it has a great deal of charm. It is Denmark's best preserved medieval town and also has some interesting museums (especially Queden's Gård). This should be your last night stop in Denmark and I would recommend the Hotel Dagmar, by the cathedral, which dates back to 1581.

DAY 11

After a morning and perhaps lunch in Ribe there only remains the drive to *Esbjerg* (20 miles). Leave the town on road 11 and then follow the signs to Esbjerg (road 24). There are clear signs to the Englandskajen and your ferry to Britain.

Guide mileages:
Esbjerg – Vejle 54 miles; Vejle – Odense 62 miles; Odense – Svendborg 46 miles; Svendborg – Haderslev 94 miles; Haderslev – Tønder 99 miles; Tønder – Ribe 62 miles; Ribe – Esbjerg 20 miles.

JUTLAND ONLY

ON THIS ITINERARY YOU go north from Esbjerg, right to the tip of Jutland, keeping to the west coast, and then returning south down the eastern side of the peninsular.

Your first day's drive takes you to the pleasant town of Ringkøbing and after an overnight stay you continue northwards through typical Jutland scenery via Holstebro and Struer to Hanstholm.

The following day your route swings eastwards to the city of Ålborg, with its many attractions. Then it is north west again, to the area of almost endless beaches and sandhills, passing Denmark's 'little Sahara' and halting at the artists' town of Skagen.

Skagen is the most northerly town on Jutland but you will want to go the extra two or three miles to the very tip at Grenen. After an overnight stay, it is time to return southwards, crossing the Limfjord by ferry and completing the day's drive at Skørping, near the heart of Denmark's biggest forest.

There are more scenic delights to follow: along minor roads around the Mariager Fjord and to Mariager itself; then south to Randers and across the Djursland peninsular to Grenå. The following day is spent exploring the varied attractions of Djursland before spending your next night at Ebeltoft.

Århus, Denmark's second largest city, is your next destination. Here you should preferably stay two nights before resuming your southbound journey again. Your last night is spent at Vejle before returning to Esbjerg. On this final day you would have time to reach Ribe for a brief visit or alternatively, if you have children with you, to stop off at Legoland.

You can complete this itinerary with only nine nights in Denmark. Ten or eleven nights would be better as this would provide greater opportunities for local exploration.

DAY 1

Leave Esbjerg on the coast road through Hjerting and then follow signs to Billum, turning left to Oskbøl (road 431). Here you take the road that parallels the railway line to Henne Stby., where you turn left towards Henne Strand. On the left is Lake Filsø, a National Trust area, but you turn right through the Blåbjerg Plantation, a migrating dune 210 ft above sea level. You join the road (181) from Varde at Nørre Nebel, turning left towards Nymindegab. Here the road swings north with the sea on one side and the Ringkøbing Fjord on the other. Between road and sea are sandhills and meadows dotted with summerhouses and with numerous camping sites. The fjord, on the right, presents a placid picture with distant views of the opposite shore. At the south end of the fjord is the attractive Bork Havn Holiday Centre while at Tipperne there is a bird sanctuary.

Roughly halfway along this road is the fishing harbour of Hvide Sande while at the end of the fjord, at Søndervig, you turn right (road 15) to Ringkøbing, six miles to the east.

Ringkøbing (**24**) has a pleasing town centre while the local tourist office has a useful folder which guides you around the little streets with their well-preserved old houses. Hotels: Hotel Fjordgården – modern, well-appointed with comfortable rooms and on the outskirts of town. I have found it a relaxing night stop. Youth hostel. For good food try Slippen, a cellar restaurant, while I have also heard good reports about Bøffen.

At Søndervig there is a Danland holiday hotel which is only 200 yards from the wide, sandy beach (reached over the top of the sandhills). Apart from self-catering apartments it also has hotel rooms. A few miles up the coast at Husby Klit is Strandgården, a former farm and an interesting museum of interiors.

DAY 2

Take the Holstebro road (16) and, if you have children, prepare to turn right five miles north at Hee where there is one of the activity parks. Sommerland West (**24**)☆ Stay on road 16, but bear right at Ulfborg to *Holstebro* (**26**), a town which claims to be the cultural centre of western Jutland (excellent art museum). It certainly supports the arts and is a good shopping centre. Hotels: Bel Air, Hotel Royal Holstebro and Krabbes. Youth hostel.

Continue on road 11 via Struer, a modern town on the Venø Bugt. You leave the town over a causeway and soon reach the Oddesund bridge and the area known as Thy (environmentalists note the lines of electricity-producing 'windmills'). A diversion is to take a right turn to Tambohuse where the kro (inn) makes a pleasant stop for lunch. The countryside now becomes more varied and at Hurup you take a left turn on to road 545 marked to Vestervig where there is the largest village church in Scandinavia.

This secondary road goes through pleasant scenery and at Vestervig look for the left turn, in the main street, to Krik and Agger (not very clearly signed). The *Agger Tange* is a long spit of land, with water on both sides, which ends at the ferry for Thyborøn. This is a very good area for bird watching (web-footed and wading birds) and also for sea fishing. There are two modern and well-equipped self-catering holiday centres in this area: the Hotel Agger Tange and the Feriehotel Krik Vig.

Look for the minor road which takes you past Ørum Sø (lake) and Tolbøl and Ørum. Immediately after the latter village turn right and shortly afterwards turn left on the secondary road from Vestervig to Klitmøller (181). To the right you will see in the distance the Morup Mølle Kro which might be worth a slight detour for refreshments or a meal. There is excellent fishing at this Kro and the Hvidbjerg river actually runs through the inn's garden.

Continue along the secondary road to *Klitmøller* which wends its way through a nice mix of fields, woods and heathland, interspersed with small lakes and streams. A considerable amount of land in this area belongs to the Danish National Trust. Another little detour involves a left turn to Nørre Vorupør, one of the last fishing hamlets on the west coast where the boats are hauled up on to the beach. It also has an aquarium. Klitmøller, where you reach the coast, is a former fishing harbour and now a holiday village with summerhouses.

The next stretch of the road to Hantsholm runs through wild and quite spectacular scenery with the beach and sandhills on the left and the Hansted Reservat on the right. This was formerly rolling dunes which have now become a treeless heathland. It is an area rich in bird and wild life. There are no roads across it and it is closed to the public during the breeding season (April 15 – July 16).

Hantsholm, like the scenery around it, is unusual. In 1917 the Danish Government decided to build a harbour here but the work only proceeded very slowly. In World War 2 the occupying German forces made it a major fortified zone so that, with a similar fortified area in Norway, the entrance to the Baltic was controlled.

In the 1960's the construction of a new harbour and town was begun. The town plan allowed commercial, residential and shopping areas to be segregated with heath and woodland between them. The town is therefore spread out over a wide area and the harbour cannot be seen as it lies at the base of steep chalk cliffs.

There are two museums, one by the lighthouse and the other in one of the former gun emplacements. There is a good viewpoint on the cliffs, which overlooks the harbour and the sea (restaurant nearby). Hotel: Golf Hotel Hanstholm, modern and well-appointed with a good restaurant, welcoming atmosphere. On the minor road to Vigsø there is a well-located camping site.

DAY 3

The Thisted road (26) is your exit from Hanstholm, but take the left fork (road 29) to Østerild and Fjerritslev. Just short of Østerild take the left turn to Bjerget and Vust which is an alternative route to Fjerritslev. This begins as a pretty tree-lined road and later the scenery becomes much more rolling. At Bjerget you can enjoy a splendid view across the Lund Fjord (there is a useful lay-by on the left) while in the other direction there is a vista of heathlands as far as the eye can see.

A short and worthwhile detour is to take the left turn at the end of the Lund Fjord to Bulbjerg. This is a piece of limestone 130 ft high from which you have outstanding views of the area which is known as the 'shoulder of Denmark'.

At Fjerritslev turn right to Aggersund (road 29). You will

cross the Aggersund by a bridge and a few miles beyond there is a
left turn to Brøndum and Nibe. This road goes through gentle,
rural countryside and at a T-junction you will see that Nibe is
signed in both directions. Take the left-hand road which is the
longer and more picturesque route via Kølby and Farstrup which
brings you down by the water at Sebbersund. The road follows the
curve of the bay beyond which is *Nibe* (**51**), a quiet little town of
narrow streets and cottages and with a small harbour.

Continue through the town on the road (187) to Ålborg,
Denmark's fourth largest city which lies on the Limfjord.
Although it is a major industrial and commercial centre (among
the products made here is aquavit) it remains an interesting and
lively city, offering plenty to do and see (check entry **53** in the
'Attractions for Children and Adults' chapter). Hotels: Hvide
Hus (few minutes from the city centre), the restaurant, 16 floors
up, offers panoramic views. Rooms are well-equipped. Others:
Hotel Phønix, first-class, old-established and nearer the city
centre. Limfjordshotellet (close to restaurants, shops) and
Slotshotellet, both modern with well-appointed rooms. Hotel
Chagall, Park Hotel, Hotel Hafnia, Hotel Ansgar and, on the
outskirts, the Scandic Hotel and Hotel Scheelsminde. Youth
hostel. There is a marvellous choice of restaurants plus several
nightclubs and discos and for a drink with atmosphere try Duus
Vinkjælder in Jens Bangs Stenhus. A two night stay would
provide more time to explore the city and be worthwhile.

DAY 4

Cross the bridge spanning the Limfjord to Nørresundby and turn
left (roads 11/55). At Åbybro bear right on road 55. Beyond
Panderup there is a left turn to *Blokhus* (Road 559), a village of
200 inhabitants which has now grown into a major Danish holiday
centre. There is a large Danland self-catering hotel, which is a
dominant feature. Youth hostel. The wide, firm, sandy beach is
backed by sandhills and simply stretches away into the distance.

You can drive all the way along the beach to *Løkken* (**54**)
about 10 miles away – but watch out for bathers and observe the
speed limits. On the way to Blokhus you will see a sign on the left
which points to Fårup Sommerland (**55**)☆, the pioneer among the
activity parks which now has a giant Aquapark. It's a priority stop
for families.

If you don't take to the beach, return to road 55 and motor
on to Løkken which is another seaside resort with many
summerhouses, numerous hotels, self-catering centres and no less
than 11 camping sites, plus numerous restaurants. Quite appealing if the weather is good and if you like busy seaside resorts.

Returning to the main road turn left and shortly afterwards
take a right turn to Børglum. On top of high ground is a
traditional windmill and nearby the impressive white-washed bulk

of the Børglum Monastery (56). From here take the minor road to Vittrup and as you leave the monastery you will have a superb view of this entire area of Jutland.

At the main road at Vittrup turn right and then left at Sønder Rubjerg to Lønstrup. You will now see the huge sandhills at *Rubjerg Knude* (59) and if the wind is blowing (as it usually is along this coast) it will whip the sand up in an amazing fashion. Turn left down the narrow road to Rubjerg lighthouse, which is now almost hidden behind the sandhills. There is an interesting museum in the lighthouse and in an adjoining building there is a cafeteria where you get sand with everything. A highly unusual location and well worth seeing, though you will be feeling a bit sandy after your visit.

Rejoin the road to Lønstrup and continue to *Hjørring*, the ancient capital of Vendsyssel, the name given to this particular region of Jutland. It is now a modern commercial town but it retains an attractive older part which is worth a few minutes' inspection. There is an interesting historical museum of Vendsyssel in the town. Leave on the E39 to Hirtshals (62) and bear right on the secondary road via Bjergby, Uggerby and Tversted (on road 597). As you approach the main road (40) to Skagen you will see the outline of *Råbjerg Mile* (60) on your left. This is a remarkable sand desert surrounded by heathland. It is best approached on the Kandestederne road which is a left turn at Hulsig off the main road to Skagen.

As you approach Skagen you will be able to see the sea on both sides of the now very narrow peninsula. *Skagen* (61) is somewhat uninspiring to begin with, but keep going and it will improve and become much more picturesque. It has quite a large fishing harbour and the older parts of the town are very attractive and full of charm. It is one of Denmark's oldest and most distinctive resorts as well as being the 'artists town' (because of the unusual quality of the light reflected from the sea on three sides). Hotels: Brøndums (old-established and reputedly very good), Hotel Skagen (modern, on the outskirts), Hotel Inger. Youth hostel. Four camping sites in the area.

You can drive three miles beyond the town to Grenen at the very tip of Jutland. From here you can walk across the sandhills to where the waters of the Kattegat and Skagerrak meet. By the car park is a restaurant and cafeteria and an art gallery.

DAY 5

Return south on road 40 to *Frederikshavn* (58). Busy ferry port with connections to Norway and Sweden and the little island of Læsø. The Bangsbo museum is particularly fascinating and should be seen, while the Krudttårnsmuseet is also of interest. Splendid views from the 196 ft high Cloostårnet tower. Hotels: Stena Hotel Frederikshavn (modern, with a super tropical wonderland pool in the centre), Jutlandia (modern, extensively refurbished, excellent), Hoffmanns, Park, Mariehønen, Turisthotellet, Motel Lisboa.

Turn off at Sæby (**57**) and visit the Voergaard Slot, a renaissance castle from 1586 (open daily June to end August), continue south on the 541 which keeps to the coast to Asa and turn right on the 559 to Dronninglund where the castle is now an attractive hotel and conference centre. (Quiet, not suitable for children, open June 25–August 15). Return to Asa and rejoin the 541 south. The road continues to parallel the coast, although often screened by woods. At Hou there are two well-placed camping sites. Drive down to the little ferry berth at Hals for the six-minute crossing to Egense. This road (still the 541) also keeps to the coast and at Dokkedal bear right on the road through Kongenslev and Lyngby to Skørping.

Skørping is a small town on the edge of Denmark's largest forest – the Rold Skov (15,800 acres) and close to the Rebild Hills (**52**). Hotels: Rebild Park, in the centre of Skørping, close to the railway but having excellent rooms and a good restaurant with a pleasant atmosphere. Youth hostel. Not far away in the heart of the forest, is the Rold Stor Kro, built in 1958. There are fine views of the Rebild hills from the restaurant and it has a large comfortable lounge, an indoor pool and bar, sauna, exercise room and solarium. Several camping sites in the area. There are some lovely walks in the Rebild hills.

DAY 6

At the main E45 turn left to Hobro, but just before this town is reached take the left turn to Hadsund (road 541). At Valsgård take a sharp right turn in the village. This road is quite elevated and affords some good views of the surrounding countryside. Watch for a right turn to Krogen, which is a minor road, you then bear right again on to an even smaller road which soon becomes an unsurfaced track. Here you look down over the Mariager Fjord.

The track – which is quite negotiable – twists and turns through the woods and eventually passes a solitary farm and crosses a small dam. On the left is the small Kielstrup lake and on the right the fjord. At the end of the dam take the right hand track. This is a remote and quite enchanting area and worthy of exploration. The track leads you down into the tiny little village of Stinesminde with its small harbour (notice the eel traps). Take the same road out of the village but turn right at a T-junction which leads you to the Hobro – Hadsund road again at Our.

At Hadsund turn right over the bridge and then right again on the road to Assens and Mariager (555) – an attractive drive to an appealing little town. *Mariager* – the town of roses – with its cobbled streets and sleepy air is a good place to break your journey for a while. Abbey and museum. Preserved railway (**50**)☆. Hotel: Postgården – charming with good food.

Leave the town on the Randers road, along which at the little village of Hvidsten is the pretty, half-timbered Hvidsten Kro, in my opinion one of the most attractive inns on Jutland. The little rooms are stuffed with interesting bygones while the culinary speciality is a bacon omelette served in the pan. But there is another aspect to the Hvidsten Kro: in World War 2 it was one of the centres of the Danish resistance movement and the owner of the inn and a number of the villagers were discovered and subsequently shot. Their memorial is in the churchyard.

Randers (**42**), a busy commercial and industrial town, is also a good shopping centre. There are some preserved old buildings and a number of the principal streets have been pedestrianised. It is not the easiest town to negotiate by car and if you decide to stop it is best to find a car park and explore on foot. Hotels: Randers (in the centre), Scandic Kongens Ege (modern, elevated position and just outside the centre). Leave Randers on road 16 to Grenå.

Grenå (**36**) is a small town and ferry port (connections to Zealand, Sweden and the little island of Anholt). Hotels: Stena Hotel Grenaa – modern with well-appointed rooms, outdoor pool, lounge and bar. At nearby Gjerrild there is the Gjerrild Kro and Motel. Two camping sites in Grenå and several others in the area. Youth hostel at Gjerrild.

DAY 7

This day involves only a short drive to your next night stop at Ebeltoft. Alternatively you could spend two nights at Grenå or, instead, two nights at Ebeltoft. Your free time will give you an opportunity to explore the attractive Djursland peninsula. Children will probably opt for Djurs Sommerland (**38**)☆, a super activity park off the Grenå – Randers road (from Grenå take the third left turn to Nimtofte which is signed). Other places of interest include Gammel Estrup Castle (**39**) at Auning; Clausholm Castle (**40**) at Voldum; Sostrup Castle (now a convent, retreat and guest house) near Gjerrild; Meilgård Castle (now a small hotel and conference centre in beautiful surroundings and with part of the stables converted to a restaurant); and Rosenholm Castle (**37**), near Hornslet.

There are good beaches with safe bathing south of Grenå and at Bønnerup near Gjerrild, to the north. There are other castles and manor houses which are not open to the public (but which can usually be seen from a public road) such as Katholm, Rugård, Løvenholm and Skaføgård. Also runic stones at Rimsø, where there is Denmark's oldest vicarage (*c.*1593) and, near Tåstrup, a prehistoric burial site with dolmens and a passage grave.

Study the local brochures and the map and then decide on where you want to go. Ebeltoft, your overnight destination, can be reached from various directions – the shortest way from Grenå is on road 15, bearing left at Tirstrup and then following the signs.

DAY 8

One of Denmark's oldest towns, *Ebeltoft* (**35**), is now in the centre of a popular holiday area. It is on the attractive Ebeltoft Bay while the Mols country to the west, with its hummocky hills, is quite appealing. Hotels: Ebeltoft Strand (modern, by the beach); Hvide Hus (large, overlooks the bay from an elevated position); Ebeltoft Park Hotel (modern, on the outskirts); Hotel Vægtergården (at Femmøller Strand to the west of Ebeltoft); Hotel Vigen (in the centre). Youth hostel. There are eight camping sites in the area and nearby is the Øer maritime holiday centre, an imaginative arrangement of self-catering 'villages' on seven small artificial islands.

Leave Ebeltoft on the road to Rønde, via Femmøller and Egens which takes you past the ruins of Kalø Castle (on the left and at the end of a little causeway). At Rønde you join road 15 to Århus.

In spite of being a major industrial and commercial centre and having a busy harbour, *Århus* (**33**) is a very enjoyable city with a host of attractions and excellent shops – see the chapter on 'Attractions for Children and Adults'. Hotels: Marselis – lovely position by the Marselisborg Forest and facing the bay; Hotel Kong Christian d.X, very modern and more a business hotel with an excellent restaurant. Other hotels: Hotel Atlantic (large, central), Hotel Ritz (very central, by the station). Mission Hotel Ansgar (also by the station), Hotel Windsor, Eriksens Hotel and Hotel Royal (a central old-established hotel, now refurbished). Several camping sites. Youth hostel. There is a wide range of restaurants plus several nightclubs and discothèques. Because of its choice of attractions Århus really deserves a two-night stay.

DAY 9

Motor south from Århus on the Odder road (451), taking a left turn marked to Moesgård, where the Museum of Pre-History is in a former manor house. After visiting the museum (if you have the time) follow the minor road to Ajstrup and Norsminde where you cross the Norsminde Fjord by a short causeway. Here there is an attractive inn, the Norsminde Gammel Kro (which dates back to 1693), speciality fried eels.

Carry on through Saksild and Odder where you follow the signs to Skanderborg (road 445). Here you should take the old main road (170) south rather than the E45 motorway, through Skanderborg and Horsens. Continue south to *Vejle* (**18**) at the head of the Vejle Fjord. Hotels: Scandic Australia, Vejle Center (modern, good value, welcoming), Park, Motel Hedegården and the Munkebjerg, three miles along the southern shore of the fjord. It enjoys a splendid elevated position, surrounded by woods and maintains a high standard of comfort and cuisine. A good choice for your last night in Denmark.

DAY 10

Take the Kolding road out of Vejle but bear right before leaving the town on the 'Ribevej' signed to Esbjerg (417). However if you have children you should leave Vejle on road 28 to Billund and *Legoland* (**21**)☆. It is 36 miles from Legoland to Esbjerg so allow yourself sufficient time to drive to the ferry – even if you have to extricate your offspring by force.

The alternative is to continue along the secondary road to the E20. Here you can turn right for Esbjerg, but if you have two or three hours in hand, cross the main road and continue south via Foldingbro on road 32 to *Ribe* (**11**). Go into the town centre with its imposing cathedral and well preserved townscape. Ribe is 20 miles from Esbjerg so allow time for your journey to the port.

The approach to the ferry terminal is well signed whether you are coming from Billund or Ribe.

Guide mileages:
Esbjerg – Ringkøbing 62 miles; Ringkøbing – Hantsholm 103 miles:
Hantsholm – Ålborg 70 miles; Ålborg – Skagen 97 miles; Skagen – Skørping 103 miles; Skørping – Grenå 91 miles; Grenå – Ebeltoft 22 miles; Ebeltoft – Århus 31 miles;
Århus – Vejle 61 miles; Vejle – Esbjerg (via Legoland) 54 miles; Vejle – Esbjerg (via Ribe) 75 miles; Vejle – Esbjerg (direct) 58 miles.

MAINLY CENTRAL JUTLAND

CENTRAL JUTLAND includes some of Denmark's finest scenery and this itinerary not only takes you to the heart of it, but also encompasses the cities of Ålborg and Århus and the Djursland peninsula.

An indirect route from Esbjerg to Vejle occupies the first day and after an overnight stop you pursue a meandering route to and through Denmark's beautiful lake district. This is one of the most appealing areas of the country with its enjoyable mix of lakes, hills and forests.

Silkeborg is in the centre of the region; naturally that is where you pause before following another irregular course so you can see various places of interest. Your destination is Skive, and the next morning there is an opportunity to visit the fascinating open air museum at Hjerl Hede and also Spøttrup Castle. Then you take a north-easterly route across Salling and Himmerland to the busy city of Ålborg on the Limfjord.

There is time to see something of the city before heading south because your day's motoring is quite brief – to Skørping, on the edge of Denmark's largest forest, the Rold Skov. After an overnight stay you continue southwards through the pretty little town of Mariager and an unspoilt area to the south-east which is well off the tourist track. Your day's journey is completed with a drive through some of the Djursland peninsula's most delightful scenery, before reaching Grenå.

Most of the next day is available for you to explore this region with its good beaches, gently rolling countryside and numerous castles and manor houses. You stay at Ebeltoft, a picturesque little town overlooking an equally attractive bay.

Århus, where you spend your last night in Denmark, is the country's second largest city and provides plenty of opportunities to fill your time, in fact two nights here would be preferable.

Your final day follows the most direct motorway route to Esbjerg and there is ample time to reach the port before your ferry departs for England.

This itinerary involves a minimum of eight nights in Denmark, but you would certainly be able to see more by extending your stay to nine or 10 nights. An extra night at Silkeborg and Århus would be my recommendation.

DAY 1

The main Kolding/Odense road, the E20, is your exit from Esbjerg. Roughly halfway to Kolding, at Holsted, you leave the main road and turn left on to the 425. When you approach Hovborg turn right into the village and then in the centre turn right on the minor road to Vorbasse.

Just before you turn you will see on the left the attractive 150-year-old Hovborg Kro, a famous moorland inn and now considerably extended (good food). The Vorbasse road takes you through a forested area which is comparatively flat. At Vorbasse, a meeting place of five roads, bear left and then right on the road to Skjoldbjerg and Store Almstok. This takes you round the edge of Randbøl Heath, which can be seen in the distance to the right.

When you reach the secondary road (176) from Egtved to Billund you turn left. As you approach Billund, turn right on to road 28 to Vejle. If, on the other hand, you have children, they will demand that you go straight on and follow the signs to Legoland (**21**)☆.

Vejle (**18**), at the end of the fjord, enjoys a splendid position with hills (and comparatively high ones for Denmark) on either side of it while to the north-west is the appealing landscape of the Grejs valley. The heavy traffic that used to come through the centre now uses the motorway that bypasses the town and crosses the fjord on a magnificent bridge. Both the north and south sides of the fjord are very beautiful. There is a big wooded area on the former, while on the southern shore the road eventually climbs steeply to Munkebjerg, 320 ft above sea level. Among the woods is the Munkebjerg Hotel, renowned for its comfort and cuisine and a great favourite of mine. At the hotel you can go for walks, borrow a bicycle, play tennis or go for a swim. Other hotels in Vejle are the Scandic Australia, Vejle Center (modern, cheeful), Park and Motel Hedegården. Youth hostel.

DAY 2

Take the Herning road (18) and pause at Jelling (**19**) to see the two huge burial mounds and the runic stones in the churchyard. One of the stones depicts the crucifixion and because it tells of the introduction of Christianity to Denmark it is often called Denmark's birth certificate. Continue to Givskud where there is a large safari park (**20**)☆ where you can drive for five miles among the animals: camels, llamas, elephants and up to 40 lions. Here you turn right on to a minor road through Nørre Kollemorten to road 13, where you turn left to Nørre Snede, this road taking you through a wooded area. In Nørre Snede take the right fork to Bryrup and Silkeborg (453).

On the way to Bryrup the scenery is not very interesting, but at the end of the village turn left to Vrads when there is a marked change as this little road winds up and down through hills and woodland. Just short of Vrads, on the left, is the end of the Bryrup-Vrads preserved railway (**29**)☆ The station building is now a small restaurant. In Vrads village look for the sign to Asklev and take this minor road which crosses Vrads Sande, an extensive moorland area. Originally it was fertile ground but it was destroyed by drifting sand in the 17th century.

Right turn at Asklev on to the road to Them, which continues through pleasant country before you turn left to Rodelund. There is a staggered crossroads at Rodelund and you need to make a right and a left turn in order to gain road 445 to Ry and Himmelbjerget. It is along this road that you turn left to get to one of Denmark's most scenic viewpoints: Himmelbjerget or 'heavenly mountain'.

There are plenty of walks in the area but the most popular one brings you to the tower, built in 1875, on the summit. From this point there are magnificent views over the lakes and surrounding countryside.

Return to the Ry road and when you reach this little town take a left turn immediately beyond the railway crossing followed

by another left turn signed to Laven. This road through Laven to Silkeborg is most attractive with views of the lake on the left and the distant hills beyond. At Laven you can turn down by the lake for a short pause to take in the scenery. A little further on is the Terrassen Restaurant, on the right, which has a splendid outlook. There are several good camping sites in the immediate area.

In *Silkeborg* (**28**) turn left to reach the town centre. The heart of the town is pedestrianised but there are plenty of peripheral car parks. Don't forget to visit the museum and see the head of the 2,200-year-old 'Tollund Man' – slightly macabre but fascinating. You can also take trips on the lake on the splendid little paddle steamer '*Hjejlen*', built in 1861 and still going strong. Hotels: Dania (central), Impala (modern, just outside the town centre on road 15 with a nice position overlooking the lake. Good, but quite expensive, restaurant) and Scandic Hotel Silkeborg.

DAY 3

Leave on the road passing the Langsø (lake) on the left but instead of joining the main Herning – Århus road (15) continue straight on, through Voel. At Skannerup turn left to Gjern and on reaching this village turn right to the Jutland Car Museum (**30**)☆. Now, you may not be particularly interested in old motor cars but this museum is worth a visit just to see the quality of the exhibits. The museum is virtually the work of one man and his family.

Head now for the Århus – Viborg road (26) and turn left. This takes you past the Tange lake (good lay-by on the right, camping site and youth hostel on the left). You can deviate and turn off right along the lake to visit the Elmuseet Tange (**41**) otherwise continue through Rødkærsbro to *Viborg* (**32**). This is a town on a hill which dips down to two small lakes, the Nørresø and Søndersø. If you want a break there is a park by the Nørresø.

Leave town on road 16 towards Holstebro and after about eight miles turn right to Mønsted where you will find the Mønsted Limestone Mines (Kalk Gruber) **31**☆. You can go down into the disused mine workings, parts of which are now used to mature tons of cheese. Limestone was first extracted from this area in the 10th century and, among other things, was used in the building of Ribe Cathedral.

Return to the main road and when you reach Sjørup turn right to *Skive* (road 186). The town has no particular attractions but it makes a useful overnight stop. Hotels: Gl. Skivehus (old established, on a busy crossroads and by the river, food in the restaurant is excellent and the service brisk and cheerful). Hilltop (modern, just outside the town, elevated position, good food).

DAY 4

Your route begins on road 189 to Hvidbjerg but before you have cleared the town turn left on the 34 to Estvad. Keep to this road until you see the sign on the right to Hjerl Hede and Sevel. Hjerl Hede (**43**)☆ is a remarkable and extensive open air museum with over 40 authentic buildings, plus a stone age settlement, on a 40 acre site. They give a good impression of how people lived and worked in the past. There is a forestry museum and you can also see how peat was extracted and processed.

The museum covers only a fragment of the 2,500 acres of National Trust land that makes up Hjerl Hede, considered to be one of Denmark's most impressive untouched natural areas and which is bisected by a large lake, the Flyndersø.

On leaving the museum follow the signs to Sahl and Ål until you reach the 189 and turn right. At Sønder Balling turn left on the 573 to Rødding but before you get there Spøttrup Castle is signed to the left along a minor road. If you study the map you will see that there is an alternative way round leaving the 189 and heading for Ejsing. You can continue along minor roads around Venø Bay (Bugt). This is a convoluted way of getting to the castle but it is a pleasant meander, although I must admit I did get slightly lost at one stage. The double-moated castle (**44**) *c.* 1500 also has a small renaissance garden with medieval herbs and medicinal plants.

Return the way you came turning left to Rødding and right to Krejbjerg and continue on this minor road until you reach a T-junction. Turn left and when road 26 is reached shortly afterwards turn right but almost immediately take the minor road on the left to Roslev (very pleasant inn – the Roslev Kro – good for refreshments or lunch). At Kirkeby turn right and follow the signs to Sundsøre (road 591). If you have time you should continue north from Kirkeby to Branden and take the ferry to the little island of Fur (five minute crossing). This has steep moler clay cliffs and also an interesting museum.

Returning to the original route, at Sundsøre you take the ferry to Hvalpsund (crossing time 12 minutes). On leaving the ferry the road climbs quite sharply from the little harbour and the countryside also undergoes a change being softer and more varied. If you want you can turn right at Hvalpsund to Hessel where there is the last fully thatched manor house. Most of the buildings are 300 years old and now form part of an interesting museum of interiors and agriculture. Your route is through the Himmerland area via Farsø and Hornum on road 187, crossing the 29, and on through Bislev to Nibe (**51**), a picturesque small town on the Limfjord. Have a look at its narrow little streets and pretty cottages before continuing to Ålborg (road 187).

Ålborg has always had the reputation for being a lively city (**55**) and it does offer the visitor a variety of attractions and entertainment (see the entry in the chapter on 'Attractions for Children and Adults'). One thing which is enjoyable is a stroll through the old parts of the city and the tourist office has a useful little folder – 'Good Old Ålborg' – which takes you on a guided tour. Hotels: Hvide Hus, just out of the centre, in a park; Phønix, old-established, first class; Limfjordshotellet and Slotshotellet, both modern and central. Also Chagall, Park Hotel, Hotel Scheelsminde and Scandic (on the outskirts), Ansgar. Youth hostel.

DAY 5

As your journey is comparatively short, you could spend the morning in Ålborg before leaving. You turn on to road 595 towards Egense on the fringe of the city and turn right on to road 507 to Hadsund. Beyond Fjellerad bear right and follow the signs to Skørping. Nothing of exceptional note along this road but it is preferable to taking the main E45.

Skørping is on the edge of the Rold Skov forest and close to the Rebild Hills (**52**). Make a point of going to the latter which offer some splendid views and are quite a surprise in a country which is supposed to be nearly flat. Two other short excursions you can take are to Thingbæk Kalkminer and to Store Blåkilde. The former is an old limestone mine, close to the main E45, and in the galleries are more than 100 sculptures by two famous Danish artists, Bundgård and Bonnesen. Store Blåkilde (the Big Blue Spring) is off the Skørping – Astrup road and is a crater from which a reputed seven million gallons of water bubble up every 24 hours. The Rebild Park hotel has comfortable rooms, and a good restaurant (but is close to the railway). A few miles away, in the forest, is the Rold Stor Kro, which is a very attractive resort hotel. There are fine views from the restaurant and there is a comfortable lounge and an indoor pool. Youth hostel and camping site near Skørping.

DAY 6

Make for the E45, turn left towards Hobro. Descend into the town and on leaving turn left on the road to *Mariager* (555). Often called the town of roses, Mariager is a quiet little place with its cobbled streets. Down by the harbour is the terminus of the Mariager – Handest Veteran Railway (**29**)☆, another of Denmark's preserved railways.

Continue on the road to Assens which affords some very good views across the Mariager Fjord. Just beyond Assens bear right on the minor road through Falslev and Norup to the Hadsund – Randers road (507) where you turn right. About three miles along this road turn left to Havndal where you bear left to Klattrup. At the latter you again keep left and follow this meandering little road past Overgård, an attractive manor house which is well-screened by trees (not open to the public). This road now doubles back to the village of Udbyneder. You get some nice views along this road which is a tranquil out of the way area but having a distinct appeal of its own.

From Udbyneder follow the sign to Dalbyneder where you turn left and at a minor crossroads turn left again, this road being marked to Udbyhøj. Here you take the ferry across the mouth of the Randers Fjord (crossing time five minutes).

It is equally quiet on the south side of the fjord and when you reach Udby, take a left turn to Ingerslev where you are now much closer to the sea. You pass Estrupland manor house with its big adjoining farm buildings and continue via Store Sjørup and Hevring. A few miles beyond the last named village you reach the Allingåbro – Grenå road (547) near Vivild and turn left.

This road takes you through rolling farmland and wooded areas and there are several camping sites to the left of the road which must be quite close to the coast. Watch for the sign on the left to Meilgård and Bønnerup Strand. This is a pretty little road which leads you to the white-washed Meilgård Castle. It is now a small hotel and conference centre. There is a restaurant in the former stables.

Bønnerup Strand is a seaside village with a good beach and safe bathing (suitable for children). At the small harbour there are boats for hire which will take you out for some good fishing or you can try your luck from the shore. There is a self-catering holiday centre here. Follow the signs to Gjerrild, a pretty little village with its limestone church dating back to the 12th century. The interior has some beautiful frescoes. Gjerrild Kro and Motel and a youth hostel. Nearby is Sostrup Castle which is now a convent, retreat and guest house and is worth looking at.

Follow the signs into *Grenå* (**36**), a small town and ferry port (connections to Zealand, Sweden and the little island of Anholt). Good beaches to the south of the town. Hotels: Stena Hotel Grenaa. Two camping sites in Grenå. This itinerary is based on staying one night here and one night in Ebletoft but you can just as well stay two nights at either of these centres.

DAY 7

This day gives you an opportunity to see something of the Djurs area. There are several interesting castles, manor houses and museums such as Gammel Estrup Castle (**39**), Clausholm Castle (**40**) and Rosenholm Castle. For children there is the marvellous Djurs Sommerland (**38**)☆ which I thought was extremely well run and entertaining. Get some of the local brochures from the tourist offices in Grenå or Ebletoft – you will find plenty to occupy your time.

Ebeltoft (**35**) is an attractive small town which still retains some cobbled streets and enjoys a beautiful location on a semi-circular bay. There is also a ferry connection from here to Zealand. Hotels: Ebeltoft Strand (modern, by the sea); Hvide

Hus (enjoying an elevated position); Ebeltoft Park Hotel (on the outskirts, looks very pleasant); Hotel Vigen (in the town centre). At Femmøller Strand to the west of Ebeltoft is the Hotel Vægtergården and to the east is the new Øer maritime holiday centre on seven little artificial islands. Youth hostel. Numerous camping sites.

DAY 8

Your destination is Århus and you can either take the road to Rønde via Femmøller and Egens or make a detour through the attractive hilly Mols area, via Fuglsø, Torup, Knebel and Vrinners. Whichever route you opt for, you will pass the ruins of Kalø Castle on your left before reaching Rønde and joining the main road (No.15) to Århus.

The chapter on 'Attractions for Children and Adults' has a useful entry for *Århus* (**33**) and gives you a good idea of what the city has to offer (although even this is not exhaustive, but just highlights some of the more interesting things). This is why the city really does deserve a two night stay if you have the time. Hotels: Marselis (de-luxe and enjoying a superb position on the city's outskirts by the Marselisborg Forest), Kong Christian d.X (de-luxe, modern, splendid food), Atlantic (big, in the centre), Ritz (central, comfortable), Mission Hotel Ansgar (central), Windsor, Park, Eriksens and the Royal (central, expensive). Youth hostel.

DAY 9

A journey direct to Esbjerg keeping at first to the southbound E45 motorway via Horsens and Vejle (using the bypass over that splendid bridge). At the intersection of the E45 and the E20 follow the signs for Esbjerg.

Guide mileages:
Esbjerg – Vejle 58 miles; Vejle – Silkeborg 63 miles;
Silkeborg – Skive 56 miles; Skive – Ålborg 79 miles;
Ålborg – Skørping 22 miles; Skørping – Grenå 84 miles;
Grenå – Ebeltoft 22 miles; Ebeltoft – Århus 31 miles;
Århus – Esbjerg 105 miles.

LOITERING WITH INTENT

MOST OF THE itineraries in this book are based on the assumption that you want to see as much as you possibly can of a particular area of Denmark. Time is allowed for seeing places of interest but usually your stays are limited to just one night at each town. But this itinerary is something of an exception as it includes longer stops which afford greater opportunities for local sightseeing or plain idleness. I also suggest specific hotels which have been selected both for their location and their quality.

You start by motoring across Jutland and through the island of Funen to an hotel which is in a former manor house. Here you can make a variety of excursions before moving on across the islands of Tåsinge and Langeland and on to the island of Lolland. Your base is the small town of Maribo which is roughly in the centre of the island.

From Lolland you continue across Falster and on to the island of Zealand to a particularly pleasant inn near the town of Næstved. This makes a good base from which to explore this region or you could even make a day trip to Copenhagen.

You return to Jutland via an alternative route to, and through, Funen. Your last stop is at Munkebjerg, a short distance from Vejle. Finally you motor south-westwards for a brief visit to the beautiful little town of Ribe before departing from Esbjerg for England.

The minimum stay at each centre is two nights, making eight nights in all, but it would be much better to increase the total to 10 nights. The extra nights would be spent in those areas which appeal to you most.

TO FUNEN

Going east across Jutland on the E20 from Esbjerg is not the best introduction to Denmark for the first time visitor. While it is certainly not unpleasant, it is also not very inspiring, but at least you are getting this stretch over first. Beyond Kolding you should leave the motorway (as the E20 has now become) and drop down on to the old main road (161) passing, at Taulov, the very pleasant (if unpronounceable) Kryb-i-ly Kro (inn). This will take you nearer Kolding Fjord and across to the island of Funen on the old combined rail and road bridge.

Shortly after leaving the bridge there is a wooded area with car parks. Turn right down a small road leading to Hindsgaul, a manor house with a neo-classical main building of the 'Funen School' built in 1785. It is now a conference centre and private hotel. From the adjoining car park you can walk down to the shore on Fænø Sund or through the park to cliffs to the west. You can take a longer walk round the tip of the peninsula, following an arrowed trail, and including the memorial grove to British aircrew shot down in World War 2.

Resume your journey through Middelfart (a name that

amuses the British but not the Danes), at the end of which you bear right on the road to Udby (313). The route is pleasantly rural with Euro-market-inspired large fields growing cereal crops. If you are interested in antiques and bygones divert left to Gelsted and to Hønnerup and visit Hønnerup Hovgård, returning to the 313.

Go through Assens and then at Hårby (road 323) follow the signs to Fåborg. You will pass through the little village of Faldsled, and see on the right the Faldsled Kro which is renowned for its cuisine (but is expensive). A little further on look for the sign on the left to *Steensgaard Herregårdspension*. A former manor house and now an hotel, it is out of sight of the road at the end of a long tree-lined drive. It dates back to 1535, although the main building is 17th century, and it lies in 27 secluded acres of parkland beside a small lake.

In spite of its substantial bulk, there are only 15 bedrooms, while there are several elegant sitting rooms in different styles of decoration. Dinner is served in the candle-lit red and gold dining room. You can walk in the grounds, play tennis or ride (stables only a few yards from the house).

Apart from the delightful atmosphere of Steensgaard, it also makes an admirable base from which to explore the south of Funen. Less than five miles away is *Fåborg* (**71**), a pleasant little town which is best explored on foot (the main street is pedestrianised). See the Vesterport, one of the few remaining town gates in Denmark; the museum of cultural history in the old merchant's house (Den Gamle Gaard); Museum of Funen Paintings and the Fåborg Museum. Just outside the town is Kaleko Mølle, an old water mill and now a museum, while at nearby Horne is the only round church on Funen.

If you take road 8 towards Kværndrup look for the sign on the left to Egeskov (**67**), Denmark's finest renaissance castle. The castle is now open to the public in summer and you can stroll round the spacious grounds and gardens and there is also an interesting vintage transport and carriage museum and a labyrinth. On the way, just beyond Korinth, there is Brahetrolleborg, a substantial manor house.

Odense (**63**), the birthplace of Hans Christian Andersen, should also be visited and there is enough there to occupy a full day without any problem. The quickest way is on road 8 to Kværndrup and then left on road 9. Definitely not to be missed is an excursion to *Svendborg* (**68**), a pleasant town which has a lovely location on the Sound.

One day should be earmarked for a trip to the island of Ærø (**70**). You can take the ferry from Fåborg to Søby or from Svendborg to Ærøskøbing (or go from one and return to the other). This is a really beautiful little island, while Ærøskøbing is quite idyllic. Marstal, the island's other town, may not be quite as

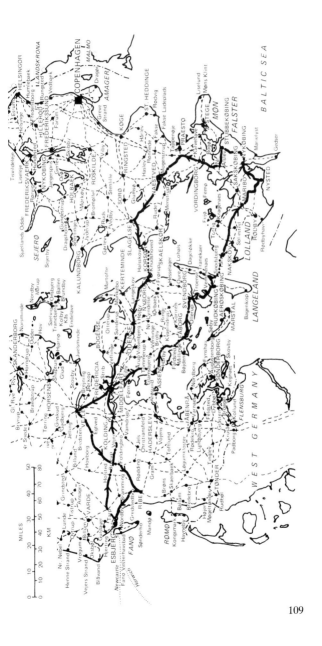

appealing as Ærøskøbing but it should not be overlooked. On a sunny day the ferry trip alone is well worthwhile.

There are other places to go in this area: such as the little island of Thurø and the bigger island of Tåsinge (**69**).

TO LOLLAND

Drive via Fåborg to Svendborg (road 44) and follow the signs to *Tåsinge* (**69**) which is reached by a lengthy bridge across the Sound. Shortly afterwards turn left to Troense, a very picturesque village with its interesting maritime museum. For refreshments try the Hotel Troense which is almost next door. Continue on the minor road to Valdemars Castle which enjoys a beautiful setting and has a museum of interiors and a good restaurant. Keep to this minor road, bearing right so that you pass Bregninge church. If the day is clear, climb to the top of the church tower, the view from which is highly rewarding. Opposite the church is an interesting little cottage museum. At the nearby crossroads turn left and continue across Tåsinge, and then by bridge and causeway to the island of *Langeland* (**72**). Bear left on the Spodsbjerg road and join the Lohals road (305). Keep to the Lohals road at Simmerbølle and enjoy the rolling rural countryside to Tranekær. At the end of this village, on the right, is the impressive shape of Tranekær Castle. You can walk round the grounds and lake and if you are seeking food and drink there is a cafeteria in the former stables or you can go back into the village and visit the welcoming Tranekær Gjæstgivergaard inn.

You can either return on the same road to Simmerbølle and then take the Spodsbjerg road or work your way back along a minor road through Stengade. At Spodsbjerg there is the ferry connection (45 minutes) to Tårs, on Lolland. Having driven ashore, continue on road 9 to Maribo. It will soon be apparent that Lolland is flat, but don't let that put you off because it does have other virtues. In the centre of *Maribo* is the Hvide Hus Hotel which overlooks a park and a sizeable lake, the Søndersø.

Between Maribo and Bandholm is Knuthenborg Park (**94**), Denmark's largest manor house park covering an area of 1,500 acres and enclosed by a granite wall, five miles long. There is also a safari park through which you can drive for 10 miles. Linking Maribo and Bandholm is a preserved railway with several vintage steam engines (**95**) ☆. From Bandholm you can continue along the road (289) paralleling the coast. At Birket the church has a wooden bell tower *c.*1350, the oldest of its kind in Denmark. Beyond Torrig look for the sign to the Reventlow Museum at Pederstrup which is dedicated to Count Reventlow who led the fight for the emancipation of the peasantry in the 1780's.

In the opposite corner of the island at *Nysted* is Ålholm Castle (**96**), the history of which dates back to the 12th century.

One wing is open to the public and this is *c*.1500 but was rebuilt in 1889. Nearby, on part of the castle estate, is the Ålholm Motor Museum ☆ which has a very fine collection of old motor vehicles. From here a replica of an 1850's steam train runs to the coast. The little town of Nysted is rather quaint, with narrow streets and old houses.

TO ZEALAND

Your route from Maribo is along the secondary road to Nysted, so you can include a visit to Ålhom Castle and motor museum on the way. From Nysted follow the signs to Nykøbing on the island of *Falster* which lies neatly between Lolland and Zealand. Take the road (E55) to Gedser and on the outskirts of the town turn left on the road to Sønder Kirkeby and just beyond the village keep to the left to *Stubbekøbing*. The latter claims to be Falster's oldest town and seems to be a quiet little place. It has an interesting motor cycle and radio museum (**91**). A climb up the church tower provides some excellent views towards the island of Møn and Bogø.

From Stubbekøbing motor on road 293 until you reach the motorway (E47/E55) at junction 43 where you turn right. The motorway crosses the Storstrømmen by two magnificent bridges and in the middle is the little island of Farø (**92**). Leave the motorway on the island (junction 42) and pause for the view and possibly visit the Danish Highway Museum (Danmarks Vej-museum) or enjoy some refreshments in the cafeteria.

Rejoin the motorway and leave it at junction 39, turning left on the 265. Look out for *Mogenstrup* and on the right side of the road you will see the Mogenstrup Kro. This inn is set back from the road and surrounded by trees and the original building is now completely overshadowed by new extensions. There is a splendid restaurant at the rear, overlooking the gardens. There are lounges, several other dining areas and an indoor pool. Altogether an impressive place to stay, offering a friendly welcome while the cuisine is of a high standard.

Within easy driving distance of Mogenstrup are several manor houses, castles and museums whilst there is another island you can visit. Less than four miles from Næstved (a commercial centre and garrison town of no great appeal) is Gavnø Manor (**86**), which is actually on a small island. This three-winged rococo building was built in 1755–58 and possesses Denmark's largest privately-owned art collection. The manor house has a beautiful setting in 34 acres of parkland.

North of Mogenstrup, near Haslev, is Gisselfeld Abbey (**87**) which, like so many other Danish castles and manors, has a splendid location. In this case it is in a 100-acre park laid out in the 1870's by an Englishman, H. E. Milner. It was here that Hans Christian Andersen found his inspiration for 'The Ugly Duckling'.

Quite near is another manor house, Bregentved, on Zealand's largest estate.

Between Mogenstrup and Gisselfeld is Sparresholm a 17th century manor house, in the farm buildings of which is a large collection of horse-drawn vehicles of all kinds. Closer to Næstved is the famous Holmegård Glassworks (**86**) at Fensmark, where you can see demonstrations of glass-blowing.

One day can be earmarked for a visit to the island of *Møn* (**90**). Take the 265 road to the quiet little town of Præstø where there are two interesting museums: the Doll's Museum 'Den lille By' and the fire engine museum.

Now drive south to Kalvehave where the Queen Alexandrine bridge gets you across to the island of Møn. Drive through Stege and on to Borre where you keep left and follow the signs to Liselund. Within the beautiful park is a romantic little chateau, often referred to as the Danish 'Petit Trianon'. Also within the park are three 18th century summerhouses, the 'Chinese House', the 'Norwegian House' and the 'Swiss Cottage'. Beyond the park and below the cliffs is the sea. Altogether a very pleasant place to pass an hour or two.

From Liselund you can drive a little further south to Møns Klint where five miles of impressive chalk cliffs rise up over 400 ft from the Baltic. A short diversion is to drive down the minor road to Klintholm Havn where there are two good fish restaurants and also an attractive self-catering holiday centre. If you are seeking a longer excursion then it is only about 50 miles to Copenhagen so a day trip is quite easy.

TO JUTLAND

From Mogenstrup take the ring road around to Næstved and then road 22 to Slagelse where you join the E20 to Halsskov. This is the ferry port for crossing the Great Belt to Knudshoved on Funen (crossing time 50 minutes). In a few years you will be able to drive across via two splendid bridges. When you are at Halsskov or Knudshoved have a look at the exhibitions devoted to this immense project.

Alternatively you can use the 265 from Næstved, via the little town of Skælskør to Halsskov. This passes another attractive inn, the Menstrup Kro, which I can recommend. From Knudshoved keep on the motorway which now bypasses Odense but then take the 161 to Vissenbjerg and then turn right on the 335 to Morud. Here you turn left and continue through Stillebæk and Harndrup. This takes you through an enjoyable slice of Funen countryside. At the approach to Middelfart you rejoin the E20 just before the Little Belt suspension bridge. Shortly afterwards follow the E133 signs to Vejle.

Keep on the main road into Vejle (avoiding the E45 motorway) and when you come down by the harbour look for the right turn to *Munkebjerg*. This road runs along the south bank of the very attractive Vejle Fjord. After about three miles the road turns inland quite steeply and actually has several hairpin bends before reaching the summit. This is where you will see, on the right, the entrance to the Munkebjerg Hotel. I have extolled the virtues of this hotel on other pages, so I will simply say that it is a very good place to stay: welcoming, comfortable with excellent food and amenities. You can walk in the woods or borrow one of the hotel's bicycles or take a swim in their pool or play tennis. The Vejle golf course is near.

In *Vejle* (**18**) you can take a boat trip on the fjord or make excursions to a number of places of interest: Givskud (**16**) for the safari park or Jelling (**19**) for the burial mounds and runic stones; or to Glud (**23**) for an interesting museum with several reconstructed buildings and many bygones and artefacts. Further afield is Silkeborg (**28**) in the heart of the Danish lake district. Leave Vejle on road 13 to Tørring, then right through Åle to Brædstrup and then left on road 52. At Rodelund turn right so you can go up to Himmelbjerget – the 'heavenly mountain' – and continue through Ry and Laven to Silkeborg. Return on road 52 to Horsens and south to Vejle on the E45.

TO ESBJERG

There only remains your return to Esbjerg. Leave the Munkebjerg in good time and take the secondary road out of Vejle via Ødsted and Egtved to Brørup, crossing the E20. At Foldingbro, join road 32 to *Ribe* (**11**). Spend as long as you can in this charming old town before motoring the final 20 miles to Esbjerg in time to catch your ferry.

Guide mileages:
Esbjerg – Steensgaard 99 miles; Steensgaard – Maribo 75 miles;
Maribo – Mogenstrup 70 miles; Mogenstrup – Vejle 109 miles;
Vejle – Esbjerg (via Ribe) 75 miles.

ACCENT ON ZEALAND

THIS ITINERARY offers some notable contrasts: large towns and minor villages, beautiful beaches and the capital city, a small island and varied scenery. You begin by motoring north-east through Jutland to Denmark's second largest city, Århus. Two nights give you time to see some of the attractions before returning south to Hov for the ferry to Samsø.

After a quick exploration of this delightful island, another ferry takes you to Zealand where your next base is Holbæk. You should spend at least two nights here although three nights would be better. You would then have time for a more extensive exploration of the surrounding district, including a visit to the cathedral town of Roskilde. Now you head towards north Zealand and Helsingør. Two or three nights will give you the opportunity to visit some of the castles, museums, beaches and lakes that are to be found in this area.

From Helsingør it is a short drive down the coast to Copenhagen where, depending on the time at your disposal, you can stay for two or three nights. Denmark's friendly capital will easily absorb all your time before heading westwards to Halsskov and across the Great Belt by ferry to Knudshoved and an overnight stay at Nyborg.

The north-east corner of Funen is explored before making for Odense. After one or two nights in this, the birthplace of Hans Christian Andersen, you return to Jutland and across the peninsula to Esbjerg.

The minimum number of nights in Denmark is 10 but it would be preferable to allow 12 or even 14 so that you can make the most of your visit.

DAY 1

For about 24 miles from Esbjerg you keep to the main E20 road to Kolding and Odense before turning left, between Holsted and Vejen on to road 417. This is a pleasant secondary road to Vejle, via Bække. At Vejle join the main road north to Horsens where you can, if you wish, steer clear of the E45 motorway and continue first on road 170 to Horsens then on road 433 through Solbjerg to Århus.

DAY 2

A day in *Århus* (33) to see some of the many things it has to offer. (See the chapter on 'Attractions for Children and Adults'). The 'Old Town', the Museum of Prehistory at Moesgård and the cathedral should be high on your list. For details of hotels see the 'Jutland Only' itinerary.

DAY 3

Take the 451 south from Århus and at Odder (which boasts

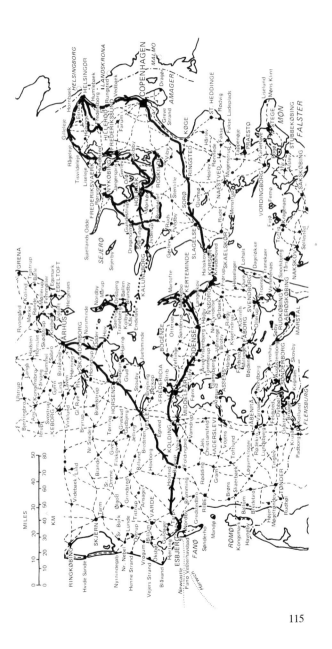

115

Europe's oldest distillery) follow the signs to Hov, a village with a small harbour and marina. From here you take the ferry to the island of Samsø (crossing time 80 minutes; make sure you have a car reservation as capacity is limited). The ferries are quite modest vessels but the crossing makes an enjoyable interlude.

Samsø (see chapter on The Smaller Islands, page 139) is a pretty little island with its undulating countryside of fields and forests. Having come ashore at Sælvig you should turn left on reaching the main road (the only main road in fact) and drive through Mårup and Nordby. The latter is particularly picturesque and after pausing there continue towards the very tip of the island at Issehoved. The road narrows and then becomes a track and when the track ends that's where you park. From this point you can walk to the cliffs or go down to the shingle and sand beach.

Returning south beyond Mårup take a left turn to the tiny harbour of Langør, which is in a lagoon. Between it and the sea is a reef, the Besser Rev. Rejoin the main road to Tranebjerg, the principal town on Samsø. The island's musuem is to be found here and should be seen. Continue through Brundby, with its post mill, to the charming village and splendid little harbour at Ballen.

Continue south through Brundby once more and take the minor road to Brattingsborg, a large villa or manor built in 1871/1898. The park is open to the public and you can also take the unmade road through the forest to the shingle beach, which is a good place for a picnic.

Follow the signs now to Kolby and then to Kolby Kås where you take the ferry to Kalundborg.

You should spend a little time at *Kalundborg* which, besides being a commercial centre and harbour, has a well preserved townscape around the imposing church with its five spires like sharpened pencil points. It was built in 1170 and is unique because of its daring construction techniques. Also near the church is the town museum. The area to the south of the town, the Asnæs peninsula, is unfortunately spoiled by a monstrous power station and oil refinery. On the peninsula is the baroque castle of Lerchenborg.

Leave Kalundborg on main road 23 and beyond Viskinge turn left to Holbæk, via Snertinge (road 155). *Holbæk* (**81**) is one of Zealand's oldest towns and it enjoys a good position on the Holbæk Fjord. There is a particularly interesting museum with many furnished display rooms in a complex of nine 17th/19th century buildings. Good shopping centre. The Strandparken Hotel, in the park on the town's outskirts, makes a good base for your stay. Excellent restaurant. Also on the southern outskirts is Tveje Merløse church – the oldest in Denmark with twin towers.

DAY 4

If you have only one free day then it is a question of choosing how you will spend it. There are several options which is why you really need a minimum of two days.

SUGGESTION 1 Drive out on the Nykøbing Sj. road (21) but quite early on take a right turn to Mårsø and Udby and continue through Løserup, Kisserup and Avdebo. This will take you right round the Tuse Næs peninsula. It is a placid, gently rolling landscape, offering lovely views of the water from time to time.

Back on the main road you are almost immediately going past the Lammefjord on your right. There is a dam alongside the road and if you stop (there are lay-bys) you can climb to the top and see that the water level is higher than the land. All the ground to the left has been reclaimed – the most major land reclamation project outside Holland. Just beyond the end of the dam, on the right, is Gundestrup Færgekro – the ferry inn – which is where in pre-reclamation days the ferry crossed the fjord.

You can keep to the main road or alternatively turn right through Nørre Asmindrup which brings you right down by Nykøbing Bay. The minor road keeps to the coast all the way into the town. Nykøbing Sj. (82) is unexceptional apart from the Anneberg Collection – a large private collection of antique glass and quite an interesting museum. If you take the road to Rørvig (ferry to Hundested) and turn left, past Rørvig church (painted a distinctive shade of yellow), you will reach a superb stretch of beach with very fine white sand. It shelves gently and is ideal for children.

An alternative way back is to take the secondary road (225), south of Nykøbing Sj., but first you may wish to deviate to Højby to see its church with its well-preserved frescoes. Drive via Høve and Fårevejle, crossing road 155 at Snertinge and road 23 at Jyderup. You will pass on the left the long drive up to Dragsholm Castle, which is now an hotel and restaurant, although the house and park are open to visitors. The Earl of Bothwell, husband of Mary, Queen of Scots, ended his days here as a prisoner in 1578 (obviously not a paying guest). His body is buried in Fårevejle church.

On the outskirts of Jyderup is a large and very pleasant park complete with woodlands and lake (well-placed camping site nearby). Further south is the Bromølle Kro, Denmark's oldest highway inn. You now take a minor road on your left which brings you through Bennebo and Torbenfeld with its church, manor house and home farm. Continue along this road (231) to Ugerløse and then follow the signs to Tølløse. Before reaching the town turn left to Tjørnede where you turn left again.

These meanderings along minor roads take you through the so-called 'Zealand Alps'. Not all that high, but quite impressive hilly scenery for Denmark. You should emerge on to road 57 at Igelsø, where you turn right for the short drive back to Holbæk.

SUGGESTION 2 Leave Holbæk on the road to Roskilde but

don't join the motorway (roads 21/23), instead keep to the old main road (155) and watch for signs on the right to Lejre and Ledreborg Castle. This takes you down an imposing tree-lined avenue, nearly five miles long. Ledreborg (1741/50) enjoys a magnificent setting, the main building standing on the edge of a slope with the grounds reaching in terraces to the bottom of the valley and then rising again. The castle and grounds are open to the public. About two miles beyond the castle is the Lejre Research Institute – an historical and archaeological research centre where Denmark's past has been reconstructed. A walk round the site (about two miles) takes you through an iron age village, a stone age working exhibition, past the sacrificial bog and the cultic dance labyrinth of the bronze age, to other examples from the past: weaving and pottery workshops, farmhouses, a forge and so on. Return by the same route to the main road and follow the signs into *Roskilde* (**80**).

Dominating Roskilde's skyline is the cathedral, for centuries the burial place of Danish kings and queens. They are entombed in amazingly elaborate sarcophagi while the light, high vaulted interior of the building is most impressive. Next in importance at Roskilde is the superb Viking ship museum down at the edge of the fjord. You can see the fully restored Viking ships – all 900 years old – as well as watching work being carried out on others under restoration.

There is also the Roskilde Museum in a former merchant's house and in which there is a fine collection of Hedebo embroidery and folk costumes. More unusual is Brdr. Lützhøfs Eftf., which is a shop restored to its appearance in 1910-20. You can look round and also buy merchandise typical of the period. From Roskilde you return to Holbæk on the main road.

This does not by any means exhaust the attractions of the area. You can visit Lake Tissø – Denmark's fourth largest lake. Or visit the fascinating Tramway Museum at Skjoldenæsholm (**84**) with its 30 trams and length of working tramline – all in the middle of glorious countryside. Nearby is the highest point on Zealand (400 ft above sea level) at Gyldenløveshøj. There's a useful little inn – the Kudskehuset – tucked away off the road, look for the sign. Another excursion is to take the ferry from Holbæk to the delightful holiday island of Orø (30 minutes crossing).

DAY 5

From Holbæk take the secondary road which skirts Bramsnæs Bay until you reach road 53 to Frederikssund. Turn left, and when you reach the village of Skibby, turn right along the minor road to Sønderby. The lake on the left is an important bird sanctuary, and shortly after leaving it you will see on the right Selsø church. A footpath from the car park by the church leads down to Selsø

Manor which has a most interesting interior which has hardly altered over the last 200 years.

Continue north through the picturesque village of Skuldelev and rejoin road 53 at Gerlev. Instead of turning right over the bridge to Frederikssund, go straight on through the forest with frequent glimpses of the Roskilde Fjord on your right. You come to *Jægerspris*, a rather long straggling little town at the end of which is Jægerspris Castle (**79**). Originally a medieval castle, it was subsequently rebuilt by various Danish monarchs. Part of the castle and the park are open to the public. Close by is the Slotskroen, an attractive inn.

Beyond Jægerspris the road continues to the end of the Horns Herred peninsula at Kulhuse where there is a short (eight minutes) ferry link to Sølager, near Hundested. Return to the road junction south of Jægerspris and cross the bridge to Frederikssund which is an industrial town. Turn left and follow the signs to Frederiksværk, which you ignore as this is also an industrial centre. Follow the signs to Ramløse (road 205).

This road goes round the northern end of the Arresø, Denmark's largest lake and originally part of the Roskilde Fjord. The area is quite heavily forested and very attractive. Before you get to Ramløse turn left on a minor road to Tibirke, Tisvilde and Tisvildeleje. This also takes you through a forested area which continues on the left hand side all the way to Tisvildeleje, which is a pretty little holiday resort. It may well get overrun with visitors in the peak summer months because by the excellent sandy beach is a car park of immense proportions – after all it is not that far from Copenhagen.

On leaving, turn left along the minor road which hugs the coastline. There are very many summerhouses along here all the way through Rågeleje to Gilleleje. Near Rågeleje is a big open stretch of heathland and a good camping site. This part of Zealand is a popular holiday area with the Danes, hence the many summerhouses, some of which are now occupied all the year round.

Gilleleje is also very much a resort even though it has a fishing harbour. The museum tells the history of fishing in this part of Denmark. Although quite pleasant, it has become rather built-up and the same goes for the next seaside town, Hornbæk. In spite of this 'urbanisation' the coastline remains attractive and the road keeps close to the sea all the way to Helsingør.

DAY 6

Helsingør (**78**) and its surrounding area really deserves more than a two night stay. The town was, for over 400 years (1427-1857), a rich source of income for the Kingdom of Denmark as all ships passing through the Sound had to pay dues. Guarding this lucrative stretch of water was the impressive bulk of Kronborg

Castle which is now the town's number one attraction (see the chapter on 'Attractions for Children and Adults'). Today it is a very busy road and rail ferry port with an intensive service to Helsingborg in Sweden. It only takes 25 minutes for the crossing so a quick visit is no problem.

There are other attractions in and around the town: the Øresund Aquarium, the Town Museum, Saint Olai Cathedral, the Marienlyst Castle, originally a summer palace (1587) and now part of the local museum and the Technical Museum. The latter is in two parts at opposite ends of the town. Helsingør has many old houses and streets and these are being restored.

Hotels: Marienlyst, by the sea on the outskirts of the town and forming a large, if rather incohesive, complex with 220 rooms and 68 holiday apartments. Vast indoor pool with wave making machine, sauna, health studio, casino and sun deck. Other hotels: Skandia, Hamlet. At nearby Snekkersten are the Scanticon Borupgaard and the Pension Brinkly. At Hornbæk there is a large modern resort hotel, the Trouville. Youth hostel at Helsingør.

During your stay you should drive out and visit Fredensborg Palace (**77**) completed in 1722, and the spring and autumn residence of the Danish Royal Family. The beautiful park with its views over Esrum lake is open all year round while the palace is only open in July. Only a few yards from the gates is the Store Kro, a large and very superior inn with period furnishings and prices to match.

Not far away from Fredensborg is *Hillerød* which has grown up around Frederiksborg Castle (**76**). The country's most magnificent renaissance castle, it was built on three small islands in a lake and enjoys a particularly beautiful setting. The castle now houses the Museum of National History. Plenty of places to eat and drink in the vicinity while the Slotsherrens Kro is actually within the castle complex.

After visiting Hillerød, drive through the Gribskov (forest) which lies on one side of the Esrum lake and return to Helsingør via Gurre, passing the ruins of Gurre Castle.

DAY 7

The most enjoyable drive from Helsingør to Copenhagen is along the coast road (152) past a succession of small towns which are strung together all the way to the capital. At Humlebæk visit the Louisiana museum of modern art which is in a beautiful old park overlooking the Sound (**75**). While at Rungsted is the fascinating Karen Blixen Museum (**74**).

DAY 8

Copenhagen offers the visitor a wide choice of things to do and see, and some of the more important appear in the separate chapter on the capital. But even this barely does the city justice. Time will be your limiting factor, so select what appeals to you most and let the rest wait for subsequent visits.

DAY 9

Take the line of least resistance, in other words the E47/E20 motorway, making sure you keep to the latter when they split. If the Vikings have grabbed your imagination then leave the motorway at Slagelse and visit Trelleborg (85). This has the remains of a Viking settlement with the circular ramparts still visible and a full-size replica of the old living quarters. There are also traces of the original Viking village.

Only 10 miles further west is Halsskov where you take the Great Belt ferry (crossing time 50 minutes, reservation recommended) to Knudshoved on Funen. Leave the motorway a very short distance after driving ashore and follow the signs to *Nyborg* (66). Originally a medieval town, it is now an important traffic and commercial centre. The town museum, in a well-preserved half-timbered house, gives a good idea of how a prosperous merchant lived in the period 1600-1637. The town also has Denmark's oldest fortress gate (*c.*1600), while the west wing and Knudstårn (tower) of Nyborg castle are still in existence.

Hotels: Nyborg Strand (large, much extended, resort-style hotel overlooking the Great Belt. Restaurant, bistro. Friendly atmosphere, pleasant bedrooms). Hesselet (a de-luxe hotel, backed by woodland and overlooking the sea) and Missions-hotellet.

DAY 10

Your immediate destination is *Kerteminde* (64), formerly an old fishing town and the harbour for Odense. On one side is Kerteminde Bay and on the other Kerteminde Fjord. It is now very popular in summer, especially the beach to the north of the town. Good fish restaurant by the harbour with another tiny little place, which is excellent, nearly opposite. Continue north up the Hindsholm peninsula which has some very enjoyable scenery, passing one or two pretty villages. The road ends at Korshavn, while there is an unmade road to the final point at Fyns Hoved. The area is quite hilly and even has some cliffs, while the beach is shingle.

On the way back you can turn left beyond Martofte and take the narrow minor road along the coast. Where it swings inland there is a well-placed camping site. You go through Viby, a pretty village with a beautiful old church. There is a narrow unmade meandering road beyond Måle which brings you back to the road from Korshavn, just north of Kerteminde. When you leave the town turn right and at Ladby take a right turn and look for a sign to the Ladbyskibet (65). There, in a field, is a small mound where

121

on entering you will find the remains of a Viking ship in which a Viking chief was buried around 1,000 years ago.

Follow the signs to Kertinge and turn left, the road taking you past Ulriksholm Castle (on the right). Originally built for King Christian IV, it is now an hotel and restaurant. The attractive grounds with mature trees sweep down to the waters of the Kertinge Nor. After passing the castle turn left and at the T-junction bear right. This brings you to the Nyborg – Odense road (160) where you turn right. You will probably arrive early enough in *Odense* (**63**) to be able to do a little sightseeing: the open-air Funen village, or the railway museum or Hans Christian Andersen's house for example. (See the chapter on 'Attractions for Children and Adults'). For hotels see the 'South Jutland, Funen and a Sprinkling of the Islands' itinerary.

An alternative to staying in Odense is to continue round the Kertinge Nor, after passing Ulriksholm, to Munkebo where there is the attractive Munkebo Kro. It's a comfortable place to stay, with good food, and it is quite a short drive on the 165 into Odense.

DAY 11

A little time for more sightseeing or shopping before driving on the E20 to Esbjerg in time to catch the ferry to England.

Guide mileages:
Esbjerg – Århus 95 miles; Århus – Hov 18½ miles;
Kalundborg - Holbæk 27 miles; Holbæk - Helsingør 86 miles;
Helsingør - Copenhagen 27 miles; Copenhagen - Nyborg 68 miles;
Nyborg - Odense 56 miles; Odense - Esbjerg 86 miles.

FOR A SHORT STAY

IF YOU HAVE a limited amount of time at your disposal, for example a long weekend, there is much to be said for making Esbjerg your base. You can then enjoy a number of excursions to places of interest in the surrounding area as well as exploring the town itself. If you don't want to take your car you could rent one in Esbjerg or if you flew to Billund you could pick up a rental car there (it's only 36 miles from Esbjerg). If you go out of season check the availability of any short stay deals with Scandinavian Seaways or other tour operators.

ESBJERG

It might be said that *Esbjerg* (15) has been founded on fish and ships. It is Denmark's largest fishing port and an important gateway for Danish exports to Britain, while today it is also involved in the offshore oil industry. Although it is now the country's fourth largest town, in 1868 it had only 30 inhabitants and its brief history does mean that it lacks old world charm. It is a good shopping centre with a pedestrianised street stretching right across the central area of the town. Activities available in the immediate surroundings include golf, riding, fishing, rowing, bathing, windsurfing and tennis.

A link with seafaring and fishing is the Fisheries and Maritime Museum which includes a large salt-water aquarium with every kind of fish living in the seas around Denmark. The museum features a unique collection of fishing equipment, models and many other exhibits including an interesting outdoor section. There is also a sealarium.

Other places of interest are the Esbjerg Museum with its fascinating urban environment and the Printing Museum which illustrates 500 years of printing and at the same time is a working print shop. The Esbjerg Art Museum, housed in a modern building overlooking the harbour, is devoted to Danish post-1915 paintings and sculptures. It has an attractive restaurant.

On the town's outskirts is the Fishermen's Memorial Park, another indication of its close links with those who earn their living from the sea. Also in the park are the graves of Allied airmen, German servicemen and European refugees who died in World War 2.

Hotels: Hotel Britannia, just off the main square (Torvet) with well-appointed bedrooms, a good restaurant, lounge and bar. Widely used by businessmen; Scandic Hotel Olympia, modern and overlooking the harbour. Other hotels: Ansgar (central, comfortable) and Hotel Bell-Inn. Youth hostel. Several camping sites in the area.

Restaurants now include one or two which are making Esbjerg a more interesting place in which to eat. For evening entertainment there are a few discotheques, some of which match the salty character of the town.

Six miles north is Hjerting on the coastal road along the Ho Bay. It is difficult to realise that before the development of Esbjerg this place had the principal harbour in the area. Facing the sea is the Hotel Hjerting with its restaurant specialising in fish dishes. A little further north, still on the coast, is the Mårbæk Plantage, a designated open space and characteristic of west Jutland scenery.

EXCURSION SUGGESTION 1

Drive out through Hjerting, follow signs to Kokspang and Billum. Turn left at Billum to Oskbol where you turn right along a minor road parallel with the railway. At a T-junction, turn left on road 465 to Henne Strand where there is a good beach. Alternatively, before you get there, turn right through the Blåberg Plantage where there is a 210ft high migrating dune which was shaped by sandstorms in the 16th and 17th centuries.

When you reach road 181 turn left through Nørre Nebel to *Varde* (**12**). Have a look at the Miniby which shows what Varde looked like in 1800. There is also the Artillery Museum and, for children, the Varde Sommerland☆. From Varde take road 12 back to Esbjerg.

EXCURSION SUGGESTION 2

It isn't essential to have children with you when you visit *Legoland* (**14**)☆ as there is plenty to fascinate adults. If on the other hand you have children, then a visit will rate the highest priority. Leave town on the E20 and a few miles out take the left fork on to road 30 to Grindsted. Bypass the town and follow the signs to Billund, where you can't miss Legoland (it's next to the airport).

There are imaginative landscapes, towns, villages and harbours all made with millions of Lego bricks. There's a wild west town (Legoredo), Legocopters, Piratland, safari cars, a timber ride and even a traffic school where your offspring can learn the rules of the (Danish) road. Fabuland is for younger children and there are numerous other outdoor pleasures and more attractions indoors. Catering facilities are excellent.

Almost adjoining the nearby Billund airport is the Center Mobilium☆ – a splendid museum devoted to aircraft, cars and rescue and salvage vehicles. The superb modern building houses a wonderful variety of full-size exhibits. Outside there is a line-up of military aircraft including very modern looking jets plus a Caravelle airliner.

Return to Esbjerg the same way, or alternatively take the Egtved road (176) and then bear right via Skjoldbjerg to Vorbasse, passing Randbøl Heath. At Vorbasse look for the road to Hovborg and turn left in the village. You will see the inviting Hovborg Kro which is a good place to pause for refreshments.

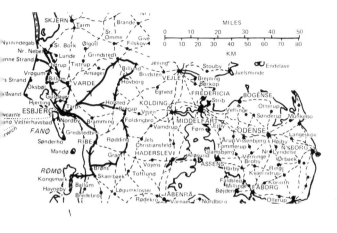

Leave the village and turn left to Holsted (road 425) where you join the E20 (turn right) to Esbjerg.

EXCURSION SUGGESTION 3

Leave Esbjerg on road 24 to *Ribe* **(11)** and watch for signs into the town. In the centre is the impressive five-aisled cathedral. A climb up the tower is tiring but offers rewarding views. Ribe's preserved townscape is really splendid with its little streets, courtyards and lovely old houses.

Ribe is well endowed with museums: The Bishop's Residence – Hans Tausen's House – is now an archeological museum and the art museum has works by artists from Denmark's 'golden age' of painting. To me the most fascinating museum is Quedens Gård, a four-winged half-timbered merchant's house c.1580 which illustrates the long and eventful history of the town.

Saunter along the little quay, Skibbroen and call in at the old Sælhunden inn for refreshments. By the cathedral is the Hotel Dagmar with its 16th century atmosphere and modern comforts. On the other side of the cathedral is Weis' Stue, one of Denmark's oldest and smallest inns, c.1600.

For something unusul take the tractor bus to the small island of *Mandø* **(12)** where the 'road' is only negotiable at low tide (don't try to drive there yourself). Mandø has a little church and a museum.

From Ribe, continue south to the island of *Rømø* **(10)** – 10½ miles long, three miles wide and reached along a six mile causeway. It is a mix of moorland, sand dunes and woodland. Good beaches on the west coast.

125

If you want to return by an alternative route, continue on road 175 after leaving Rømø until you reach the 25 at Toftlund. Turn left, drive via Gabøl to *Jels* (**13**) where there is the Orion Planetarium and Observatory. From here, turn left on to the 403 to Vejen and the E20 (left again) and return to Esbjerg.

EXCURSION SUGGESTION 4

Opposite Esbjerg, and noticeable when you arrive by ship from Britain, is the island of *Fanø* (**14**) which is reached by one of the small ferries from Esbjerg harbour (20 minute crossing). The size of the ferries effectively limits the volume of cars that can invade the island. In summer you can wait hours to get across with your car (in either direction) as there are no advance reservations – so don't plan a tight schedule. Incidentally you can only buy return tickets to Fanø.

The Ferry arrives at the 'capital' of the island, *Nordby*, which is a small town with narrow streets. On the west coast of Fanø is a magnificent beach with miles of superb sands, backed by sandhills. In spite of the low-lying nature of the island it does have scenic variations with moorland, heath and forest. At the south end of Fanø is the gem of the island: the little village of *Sønderho* with its distinctive thatched cottages. In the past Sønderho was a much more active place, building sailing ships and having a busy harbour. It is now very quiet, the harbour is silted up and tourists provide the activity.

In the village is one of Denmark's oldest inns, the Sønderho Kro which opened in 1722. It has a small number of beautifully decorated bedrooms while the charming beamed restaurant offers excellent cuisine.

There are a few holiday hotels on the island including Fanø Krogaard (Nordby), Kellers Hotel (at Fanø Bad) and Hotel Sønderho (Sønderho). There is also the Feriehotel Vesterhavet, a self-catering centre at Vesterhavsbad. Nine camping sites.

A 300-year old house is the home of Fanø Museum at Nordby which depicts the life of a seafarer in bygone days. There is also the Fanø Maritime and Costume Exhibition at Nordby which features ship models and costumes, while Hanne's Hus at Sønderho, is the best preserved example of a typical Fanø house. The Sønderho seaman's church built in 1872 includes some beautiful ship models.

Guide mileages: Esbjerg – Rømø 40 miles; Esbjerg – Ribe 20 miles; Esbjerg – Billund 36 miles; Rømø – Jels – Vejen – Esbjerg 75 miles.

OTHER CHOICES

In this chapter I have outlined some further suggestions for itineraries. They include a lightning tour of Denmark for those whose time is limited; a tour which begins and ends in Germany; and a journey along the Green Coast Road.

LIGHTNING TOUR OF DENMARK

If you have only a few days to spare and wish to make a fleeting tour of Denmark then this is the itinerary for you. You start from Esbjerg on the main E20 eastwards and beyond Holsted turn left on the 417 on which you remain until you reach Ødsted. Turn left on the 441 and a little way north of Bredsten turn right on a minor road to *Jelling* (**19**) the ancient seat of Danish royalty and after looking at the runic stones and burial mounds join road 18 to *Vejle* (**18**).

Stop for a brief look at Vejle before joining the E45 north for a short distance until you turn left at junction 59 when you are on road 13 to Nørre Snede. Here you turn right on 453 through Løve and Bryrup turning left on to the 52 and later right on the 445. You should look for the sign to Himmelbjerget (on your left) and there should be time enough to drive up and park the car and walk up to the tower for a magnificent view.

Rejoin the road to Ry, cross the railway, turn left and then left again to Laven. This is an enjoyable road all the way to *Silkeborg* (**28**), your first overnight stop (see 'Mainly Central Jutland' for hotel information). On day two take road 15 to *Århus* (**33**). There are plenty of things to see in Denmark's second largest city but as your time is limited make for Den Gamle By (the Old Town). Directions: cross the ring road, go down Silkeborgvej and watch for signs on the right.

Return to the 15 and follow the signs to *Ebeltoft* (**35**) which is at the end of road 21. This is your overnight destination and you can enjoy a stroll round this attractive little town on the bay if nothing more. (see 'Jutland Only' for details of hotels).

On day three you start with a short drive to the ferry terminal for the 90 minute crossing to Sj.Odde on Zealand (I recommend you make a reservation – see 'Internal Ferries' chapter). On Zealand you are again on road 21 and you stay with it to *Roskilde* (**80**). Visit the magnificent cathedral and the Viking Ship Museum before rejoining the 21/23 – which is now more of a motorway – to Copenhagen. Two nights are allowed for the Danish capital and what you see during your 'free' day depends very much on your personal taste.

Check the chapter on the Danish capital and among the options are: a coach tour of the city (easier than taking the car), a boat trip round the canals and harbour, a visit to *Helsingør* (**78**) for a look at Kronborg Castle and, of course, an evening at Tivoli.

It is day five when you leave Copenhagen on the combined E47/E20. You keep to the E20 when the roads split and continue across Zealand to Halsskov for the ferry across the Great Belt to Knudshoved in Funen (crossing time 50 minutes, reservation recommended). Keep to the motorway until you see signs into Odense centre (junctions 50 or 51 are probably the best).

Odense (**63**) is your last night stop and you should arrive early enough to do some sightseeing: a visit to the open air Funen Village, or Hans Christian Andersen's house for example. (For hotels see 'South Jutland, Funen and a Sprinkling of Islands' itinerary). There is time for a little more sight-seeing or shopping on day six before rejoining the E20 and after crossing the splendid Little Belt suspension bridge you are back on Jutland. From here you stay with the E20 west to Esbjerg. You will have seen a fair slice of Denmark without too much rush – enough to make you want to return for a more leisurely visit.

A DIFFERENT APPROACH

This itinerary begins in Germany. You can drive from the channel ports or take the Scandinavian Seaways ferry from Harwich (also Newcastle in summer) to Hamburg. From the latter take motorway 1/E22 which bypasses Lübeck (when the E22 becomes the E47) and goes through Oldenburg, over the Fehmarn bridge on to the island of Fehmarn to Puttgarden. Here you take the ferry (one hour crossing) to *Rødbyhavn* (**97**) and continue on the E47 but turn off at *Maribo* for an overnight stay (see 'Loitering with intent' itinerary). If you prefer you could stay at Rødby – the Danhotel is convenient.

Leave Maribo on road 153, turn right at Sakskøbing on to road 283 to *Nysted* (**96**) where there is a castle and car museum to see. Head for the 297 and *Nykøbing Fl.* (**93**). Meander along minor roads via Sønder Kirkeby, Hesnæs to *Stubbekøbing* (**91**). Take the small ferry from here to the island of Bogø from where road 287 brings you on to Møn, another island. Continue to the end of this road at *Møns Klint* (**90**). There are several places around which would make a suitable overnight stay. (try the Liselund Castle, Hotel and Restaurant in Liselund Park). Alternatively you can return across the island, keeping this time to the 59 and reaching Zealand by bridge.

At Kalvehave keep to the 265 via Præstø to Mogenstrup where there is an excellent – and much extended – inn, the Mogenstrup Kro. This would be an alternative overnight stay. Return to the E47 (junction 39) and turn left and remain on this motorway to Copenhagen. Stay at least two nights, possibly three (see chapter on Copenhagen).

Leave Copenhagen on the Strandvejen, the coast road that keeps close to the Øresund all the way to Helsingør. On the way call in and see the Karen Blixen Museum at *Rungsted* (**74**) and the splendid Louisiana modern art museum at Humlebæk (**75**). At *Helsingør* (**78**) you might like to stay overnight and visit Kronborg

Castle and perhaps take the 25 minute ferry crossing for a brief visit to Helsingborg in Sweden (I would leave your car behind).

Take road 6 to *Hillerød* (**76**) and see Frederiksborg Castle if nothing else. Now head for *Roskilde* (**80**) on road 6 where there are various places of interest – such as the cathedral and the Viking Ship Museum. Leave town on road 14 and join the E20 at Ringsted. This takes you to Halsskov and the Great Belt ferry (or the massive bridges in a few years' time).

Drive ashore at Knudshoved on Funen and join road 163 to *Svendborg* (**68**) which is a suitable place for a one or two night stay (the Hotel Svendborg is a good choice). There are plenty of things to see and do around this corner of Funen. Leave on road 44 through *Fåborg* (**71**) and turn left on to road 8 to Bøjden. Here you take the ferry to Fynshav (crossing time 50 minutes) on the island of Als.

Continue on road 8 to *Sønderborg* (**5**) and have a look at the castle. Cross by bridge on to Jutland to see *Dybbøl Banke* (**4**) which is associated with the Danish-German war of 1864. At Rinkenæs keep left along the pleasant coast road via Kollund then rejoin the 8 until you come to the E45. Turn left and within a very short distance you are at the German frontier.

The E45 (it is also motorway 7) goes south through unspectacular scenery by-passing Neumünster and on to Hamburg for either your ferry connection to the UK or else to continue south of the Elbe and on to the English Channel.

For this itinerary you need a minimum of six nights in Denmark but eight or even nine nights would be preferable.

THE GREEN COAST ROAD

The Green Coast Road is an attractive route stretching from the Netherlands through Germany and to the northern tip of Jutland in Denmark. Promoted by the International Green Coast Road foundation they have published a brochure on it and you should try the Danish, Dutch or German tourist offices in London for a copy.

This is just a brief outline of the route from Hamburg to Skagen in northern Jutland. I suggest you get a good map to check out this journey which often makes use of minor roads.

From Hamburg the route is via Itzehoe, Meldorf, Heide, Bredstedt, Niebull and across the frontier to *Tønder* (**2**). Then its *Møgeltønder* (**3**) and by a minor road to Rudbøl and Højer, across marshland country, on road 419. There is a side trip on to the island of *Rømø* (**10**) before going north on the 11 to *Ribe* (**11**). From Ribe the route is via the 24 to *Esbjerg* (**15**). Now you head for Billum, Oksbøl, Nymindegab and along road 181 parallel with the coast and the Nykøbing Fjord.

Eventually road 181 runs out of land at Thyborøn where you take the ferry (10 minute crossing) to Agger, another spit of land.

OTHER CHOICES

Keep to the 181 as it heads through woods and heathland passing the wild and deserted Hansted Reservat to Hanstholm. Now it is a mix of main road and minor roads keeping as close as possible to the coast and briefly moving inland to Fjerritslev before resorting to more minor roads to Hune and on to *Blokhus* (**54**). You can drive from here to Løkken along the sands. If you want to stick to roads, take the 55 to Løkken and on to *Hirtshals* (**62**), deviating on the way to pass *Rubjerg Knude* (**59**) and Lønstrup.

Then it is road 597 to road 40 and left to *Skagen* (**61**), the end of your journey and the end of Denmark and the Green Coast Road. The quick way south is via the 40 to *Frederikshavn* (**59**) and then keeping to the E45 all the way south to the German border just south of Padborg. From there it is still the E45 (combined with motorway 7) back to Hamburg.

Suggested night stops in Denmark: Tønder, Ribe or Esbjerg, Ringkøbing, Hanstholm and Skagen. On the return journey you could probably make do with two stops – say Århus and Haderslev. See the other itineraries on Jutland which include parts of this route and provide more information on places of interest.

THE MARGUERITE WAY

In 1990 a new tourist route was created which wanders for 2,500 miles throughout Denmark and was named the Marguerite Way – the Marguerite being the daisy-like flower which is Denmark's national emblem.

Exclusively for motorists, the route winds its way across the whole country using small roads and byways. I have not included any itineraries based on the Marguerite Way in Drive around Denmark because many of the routes were featured right from the first edition published in 1985. A case of two minds thinking alike! Of course these parts of the Marguerite Way also appear in this edition.

COPENHAGEN

INFORMATION on Copenhagen in the last edition of Drive around Denmark was prefaced by the remark that as the main purpose of this book is to take you around Denmark only a modest amount of space has been devoted to the Danish capital. I see no reason to change this approach as there are several excellent brochures issued by the Danish Tourist Board as well as other guides that concentrate on the city.

Copenhagen has several major virtues which make it particularly appealing: it is on a human scale and hasn't suffered from undisciplined development; it is easy to get around and much of the central area can be covered on foot; it is visually attractive; and it enjoys a splendid setting by the sea. In addition it has an excellent range of amenities and many places of interest. This is a city where you very quickly feel at home.

The focal point is the Town Hall Square (Rådhuspladsen) and the town hall with its 364 ft high tower. To one side is the boundary of Denmark's biggest single attraction: Tivoli Gardens. Opened in 1843 (it celebrated its 150th anniversary in 1993) it covers an area of 20 acres and is a marvellous mix of gardens, fountains, restaurants (28 of them), fun fair, theatre, concert hall, side-shows, pantomime, bandstands and much more. It has a unique atmosphere, appealing to young and old, Dane or foreigner; everyone has a good time at Tivoli.

On the opposite side of the Town Hall Square is the beginning of Strøget – five streets forming one continuous pedestrianised route, lined with shops and stretching all the way to the Kongens Nytorv (King's New Square). At the latter is the Royal Theatre, home of the Danish national ballet as well as opera and drama. Across the square is one end of Nyhavn, the stretch of water leading to the main harbour. For many years it consisted largely of seedy bars but it has now been spruced up and is mainly occupied by good restaurants.

A few minutes' walk from Kongens Nytorv is the Amalienborg Palace. It is not one building but four (built 1749–1760), one of which is the home of the Danish Royal family. When the Queen is in residence you can see the changing of the guard, Danish style, at noon. Continue beyond the palace and you will come to Churchill Park, the Danish Resistance Museum, the English church of St. Albans and the magnificent Gefion fountain. Now you are at the beginning of Langelinie which will bring you within sight of the Little Mermaid, the city's most famous statue. Returning to the centre, go down Bredgade and see the beautiful domed Marmorkirken (Marble Church).

To one side of Strøget lies the university quarter, a series of small streets with their bookshops, antique dealers, boutiques and pavement and cellar cafes. This is also where you will find the Rundtårn – a round tower which is 115ft high. You get to the top up a spiral sloping walkway (no lifts, no stairs) and Peter the

Great of Russia rode up on his horse followed, no less, by the Empress in a horse drawn carriage.

There are museums in plenty and the range of subjects is really extensive. Here is just a selection: National Museum (splendidly rebuilt quite recently and including a marvellous children's section); Ny Carlsberg Glyptotek (art – particularly Egyptian, Greek, Roman and Etruscan); Statens Museum for Kunst (primarily Danish paintings and sculpture); Rosenborg Palace (now a museum of the Royal Family); Københavns Bymuseum (presents the history of the capital); and Thorvaldsens Museum (paintings and antiques).

More varied subjects include the Danish Film Museum; the Theatre Museum; Arbejdermuseet (devoted to living conditions of the Danish people); Cafe and Øl (a restored pub – part of the previous museum – serving Danish food and beer of the 1890's); The Royal Danish Naval Museum; and – on a completely different note – the Erotic Museum (four floors of fascinating exhibits not usually regarded as museum subjects).

Places of interest which are likely to appeal to children include the magnificent Tycho Brahe Planetarium (everything from astronomy in the Middle Ages to space travel); Louis Tussaud's Wax Museum; Ripley's Believe it or Not Museum; and the Danish Toy Museum (a treasure trove of 2,500 items). On the outskirts at Hellerup is the Eksperimentarium where adults and children can try out all kinds of machines and puzzles linked to science and technology.

Of course this by no means exhausts all the possibilities – you can visit either the Tuborg or Carlsberg breweries (or both!). At the coastal suburb of Klampenborg is Bakken, a very old established amusement park with 29 restaurants and 108 different attractions. Near Lyngby at Sørgenfri, is the Frilandsmuseet, 90 acres of parkland on which there are about 100 old farms and houses with complete interiors illustrating the culture of Danish rural communities.

There is an equally large selection of churches and public buildings which are worth looking at for their architectural beauty if nothing else. The Stock Exchange (Børsen) with its famous spire of four intertwined dragons' tails is one example and Our Saviour's Church, across the harbour on Christianshavn is another. It has a staircase spiralling around the outside of the spire (you need a head for heights to enjoy it) while inside is a vast and highly ornamental organ.

The city has some nice parks and gardens, especially the King's Gardens and the Botanical Gardens. Entertainment is varied: circus, theatre, ballet, music (classical, jazz, folk and rock), cinemas, discos, some nightclubs while sex clubs and porno cinemas are still around although they are much less in evidence than in the past.

COPENHAGEN

The seaside is right at the city's front door and you can easily go across to Sweden on a hydrofoil for an hour or two. You should take a trip on one of the launches that sail through the canals and out into the harbour, while a city sightseeing tour by coach will let you see all the principal sights without the effort of driving and parking.

There is a good network of bus and local train services (S-trains) and the Copenhagen Card is a worthwhile purchase. This provides unlimited travel on buses and local trains within the metropolitan region (which, for example, stretches all the way to north Zealand) and free entry to a large number of museums and places of interest; you also go half price on the hydrofoils to Sweden. The cost (1993 prices) is Dkr 120 for one day, Dkr 200 for two days or Dkr 250 for three days (half price for children).

A useful free publication is Copenhagen this Week which lists restaurants in different categories and contains the opening hours and other details of museums and places of interest and special events. Hotels usually have copies at reception or you can get one at the tourist information office.

When it comes to food and drink Copenhagen has a very wide range of restaurants, cafes, pubs and bars to tempt the visitor. Scala, opposite the main entrance of Tivoli Gardens, is a major entertainment complex with five floors of restaurants, cinemas, boutiques and Denmark's biggest discotheque (all aimed principally at the young).

Hotels cover the whole spectrum of accommodation from small, simple establishments to the de-luxe category. The latter include the Royal (near Tivoli), Scandinavia (off-centre), D'Angleterre (traditional, Kongens Nytorv), Sheraton (10 minutes' walk from Town Hall Square) and Phoenix (near the Amalienborg Palace).

A few examples of other hotels are: Nyhavn 71 (skilful conversion of an old warehouse), Imperial (central, own parking), Plaza (by the station and Tivoli), Opera (opposite the Royal Theatre), Sophie Amalie, Admiral and the Neptun (all near the harbour).

Near the station is Helgolandsgade with a whole clutch of hotels, mostly in the medium price bracket and including the Hebron, Triton, Selandia, Absolon and Mayfair.

There are also hotels outside the city centre which avoid a parking problem. Among these is the Hotel Marina. The latter enjoys a good position on the coast road at Vedbæk overlooking the Sound and I can recommend it; good rooms and an excellent restaurant. There are several camping sites within Greater Copenhagen and also three youth hostels.

This has been a fleeting description of the Danish capital but sufficient for you to catch the flavour of it. Its style and character make it a highly enjoyable city.

BORNHOLM

ALTHOUGH IT IS inescapably Danish, Bornholm is an island apart. In the Baltic, 85 miles from the rest of Denmark, it is only 25 miles from Sweden. Geographically it is a delightful mixture and its rocky coastline alternates with dunes and cliffs, while inland there is a large expanse of forest covering a fifth of the island's total area.

It claims to have the best climate in Denmark and on a sunny day it is more akin to southern Europe than Scandinavia – a contrast which is reinforced by the sight of figs, grapes, mulberries and peaches growing out of doors. Because of the light it attracted many painters in the 19th century and it is an enchanting island.

The principal town is *Rønne* which has a busy centre and some attractive 19th century buildings. The Bornholm Museum and Art Gallery includes an old grocer's shop, textiles and traditional costumes and a maritime section with splendid ship models. (Open daily 1 Apr–31 Oct, Tues, Thur, Sun during the rest of the year). Erichsens Gard is a middle class house of 1807 with furnished rooms and a fine old garden (open daily 1 May–30 Sept). Kastellet, a 17th century tower is now a Defence Museum (open Tues–Sat, 3 May–30 Sept). The ashlar-built church c.1300 has a half-timbered tower.

Hotels: Griffin (140 rooms, five minutes from the town centre), Hoffmann (85 rooms, near harbour). Outside the town: Ryttergården (106 rooms, 30 apartments, 220 yards from the beach, own riding stables). Skovly (peaceful, near beach), Fredensborg (a mile out of town see description later in this chapter).

To make a circuit of the island drive north from Rønne (road 159) which goes through a wooded area and then take a secondary road to *Hasle*, a small town with a fishing harbour and with steep little streets and a jumble of buildings. there is a smokehouse museum in one of the old herring smoke houses (fishing is the island's principal industry after tourism). Hotel Herold (perched above the harbour, homely).

Continue on the Allinge road and after about a mile take the left turn to Helligpeder. You are by the water with the rocky foreshore on one side and tree-clad cliffs on the other – a delightful road passing occasional herring smokeries until it ends at Teglkås.

Return to Helligpeder Odde up a steep little lane which brings you out on the Allinge road again. Watch for the left turn to *Vang* and go down another steep lane to this pretty little village with its tiny harbour.

Back on the Allinge road once more there is another forested area and then you turn left to Hammershus, Scandinavia's largest fortified castle. It lies on a rocky plateau, overlooking the Baltic and 243 ft above sea level. It is a remarkable complex of buildings, some dating back to the 13th century, and it's worth exploring. Free access all year.

You are now near the northern tip of the island and on the left is Hammeren, a steep granite crag and a natural attraction and there are plenty of marked paths. You can also see the Opalsø – the opal-green lake.

Sandvig and *Allinge* were once two fishing villages but now they are virtually one and linked by mellembyerne (literally 'between towns'). Sandvig deserves to be called picturesque with its steep streets and colourful houses. Watch out for the street which narrows to only 6 ft 6 in.

You are now heading south through Allinge which, like Sandvig, is a holiday resort with plenty of hotels, pensions and restaurants. Hotels include Abilgård, Friheden, Hammersø Strandhotellet.

The cliff road south keeps to the coast through Sandkås and Tejn but at *Gudhjem* you come to what is arguably the most beautiful little town on Bornholm. From above, you look down on an untidy pattern of red-tiled rooftops, while narrow streets descend steeply to the harbour. The rocky coast contrasts with the colourful houses, the white smokeries, the green of the trees and the blue of the sea. The museum is in the old railway station (the railway closed in 1952). Hotels: Casa Blanca, Jantzens.

From Gudhjem motor inland to Osterlars to see Bornholm's biggest round church, 59 ft in diameter and dating from the 12th century. Round churches are a feature of the island and were built both for worship and defence (five are still in existence). Return to the coast road, travelling south-east to *Svaneke*.

This is another idyllic little township with its fishing harbour, beautiful surroundings and well-preserved houses. By the harbour is the inviting Hotel Siemens Gård (50 rooms, restaurant, large terrace and facing the waterfront). In the same location is the Østersøen (old merchant's house with modern extensions and 37 apartments).

Continue along this coastal route, southwards to Neksø, the island's second biggest town and a major fishing port. Museum with the accent on fishing.

Inland is Paradisbakkerne (paradise hills) a splendid rocky area of forests and lakes, rift valleys and National Trust heathland. Keeping to the coast you pass the holiday resort of Balka. Hotels: Balka Strand (37 rooms, 110 yards from the beach), Balka Søbad (106 rooms, eight apartments in wooded area near beach). Beyond Balka is *Snogbæk*, another fishing village.

You are now in the south-east corner of the island and keep to the coast, avoiding the inland route to Rønne. Look for the left turn to *Dueodde*. The road goes through a forest and when it ends you can walk over the extensive sandhills to the superb beach with its miles of the finest white sand in Europe. A noticeable landmark is the lighthouse, 153 ft high, and where you can climb

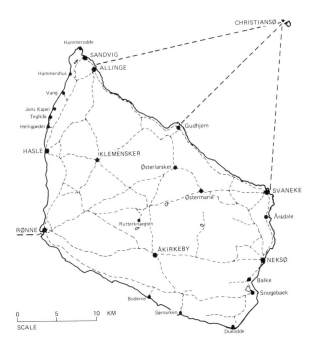

the staircase (196 steps) to the balcony at the top. From there the views are sensational and definitely worth the effort involved.

Continuing along the coast road there are numerous turnings leading down to the beach. You are now only a few miles from Rønne, your original starting point; the circumference of the island is about 100 miles.

Inland there are other attractions. Almost in the centre of the island is the extensive Almindingen forest, Denmark's third largest (5,900 acres). At Rytterknægten is the highest point on Bornholm (530 ft above sea level). A tower affords extensive views over the forest. There are numerous walks including one into the echo valley (Ekkodalen). As elsewhere on the island, there are plenty of picnic places, ample car parking, refreshment kiosks and toilets.

South of the forest is the old market town of Åkirkeby which was the island's most important centre in the Middle Ages. It has an unusual stone church c.1150.

The only other inland centres of any size are Østermarie and Klemensker which are really only large villages. The remaining

137

areas are almost entirely agricultural and provide a pleasant rural backdrop when you are motoring from one place to another.

Between Bornholm and Sweden lie some more Danish possessions – Ertholmene, a cluster of islands 10½ miles from the north-east coast. The biggest island is Christiansø where a naval base was established in 1684 which was intended to keep an eye on Sweden. It was only attacked once and that was by the British at the time of the Napoleonic war.

The most impressive buildings are the Great Tower on Christainsø and the Little Tower on adjoining Frederiksø. There are regular boat services from Svaneke, Allinge and Gudhjem.

As tourism looms so large in Bornolm's economy there are plenty of hotels, pensions, apartments and restaurants. Camping sites are also plentiful, while there are youth hostels at Rønne, Dueodde, Svaneke, Gudhjem, Sandvig and Hasle. There are three golf courses (two 18-hole, one 9-hole) and many miles of cycle tracks.

The speciality in restaurants is, of course, fish and Bornholm smoked herring is delicious while the island's smoked salmon is claimed to be the best in Scandinavia.

On my visits (and I need no encouragement to go back) I stayed at the Hotel Fredensborg, just outside Rønne, which overlooks the sea. Modern, well-furnished bedrooms, also self-catering apartments and excellent restuarants. Recommended.

In spite of catering for so many visitors (the majority of whom are Germans) the island has not lost its essential character and personality and it is a pity it is relatively unknown in Britain.

Getting to Bornholm is no problem. Modern car ferries sail nightly between Copenhagen and Rønne (plus day crossings in summer). Duration seven hours. Rostock–Rønne (7–11 hours) and Sassnitz–Rønne (3½ hours) both have one sailing a week. Swinoujscie (Poland)–Rønne (10 hours), five departures weekly. From Sweden: Ystad–Rønne (2½ hours) three to four departures a day.

THE SMALLER ISLANDS

Læsø In the Kattegat. Ferry from Frederikshavn (90 minutes). 2,700 inhabitants, 150 hotel beds, two camping sites, youth hostel. Scenery is a mix of salt meadows, heath, dunes and woodland. A distinctive feature is the use of seaweed for thatching. Two small museums. Bird sanctuary.

Fur Small island in the Limfjord. Interesting geological deposits and moler cliffs. Museum. Inn, camping site. Ferry from Branden (five minutes).

Mors In the western part of the Limfjord with bridge connections to the Thy and Salling areas of Jutland; ferries across the Feggesund (five minutes) and Næssund (five minutes). Principal town Nykøbing M. (**45**). Attractive Pakhuset Hotel. There is an interesting museum.

Varied scenery with imposing cliffs in the north. At Feggeklit there is a remarkable plateau of moler clay.

Near Sallingsund is the Jesperhus Blomsterpark (**46**) and numerous camping sites. Youth hostel at Nykøbing M.

Anholt Small island in the Kattegat with 160 inhabitants. Unique sand dune 'desert' landscape. Inn, camping site. Ferry from Grenå (2¾ hours). During the Napoleonic Wars the island was occupied by the British and became H.M.S. 'Anholt'.

Hjarnø In the Horsens Fjord. Camping site. Ferry from Snaptun (five minutes).

Endelave Between the east Jutland coast and Samsø. Camping site. Ferry from Snaptun (70 minutes).

Samsø A beautiful island between Jutland and Zealand. 4,875 inhabitants. Ferry from Hov (Jutland) to Sælvig (80 minutes) and from Kalundborg (Zealand) to Kolby Kås (two hours).

See description in the itinerary 'Accent on Zealand'. Varied scenery. Interesting museum at Tranebjerg. In the south is the picturesque little harbour of Ballen; in the north there is the pretty village of Nordby. The tiny harbour at Langør is protected by a long reef.

Hotels: Flinch's (Tranebjerg), Nordby Kro, Pension Verona (Nordby), Ballen (Ballen), Brundby (Brundby), Færgekroen (Kolby Kås). Four camping sites. Youth hostel.

Fanø The island facing Esbjerg from which the ferry sails to Nordby (20 minutes). Superb beach on the west coast. Described in the itinerary 'For a Short Stay'.

Mandø Unusual island in that it is reached from Ribe by a tractor bus at low tide. Inn. Small museum.

Rømø Linked to west Jutland by a long causeway. Varied scenery, good beaches on the west coast. More information in the itinerary 'South Jutland, Funen and a Sprinkling of the Islands'.

Als Quite a substantial island off the south-east coast of Jutland. Linked by bridge to the latter, also ferries to Funen (Fynshav – Bøjden, 50 minutes) and Ærø (Mommark – Søby, 65 minutes). Principal town is Sønderborg (**5**) which is quite appealing and a good centre. Nordborg, in the north, is dominated by industry. Augustenborg is smaller, and a pleasant little town. Enjoyable countryside.

Årø Reached in 10 minutes by ferry from Årøsund on the east coast of Jutland. Camping site.

Bagø Off the west coast of Funen. Ferry from Assens (30 minutes).

Lyø and Avernakø A pair of small islands reached by ferry from Fåborg on Funen.

Ærø This beautiful island is described in the itineraries 'South Jutland, Funen and a Sprinkling of the Islands' and 'Loitering with Intent'. Three ferry routes: Ærøskøbing – Svendborg (70 minutes), Søby – Fåborg (60 minutes) and Marstal – Rudkøbing (60 minutes).

Strynø A minor island between Ærø and Langeland. Ferry from Rudkøbing (35 minutes).

Tåsinge A delightful island facing Svendborg. Linked by bridges to Funen and Langeland. The little village of Troense is especially charming. See additional details in the itinerary 'South Jutland, Funen and a Sprinkling of the Islands' (**69**).

Thurø Horseshoe-shaped island wedged between Funen and Tåsinge. Causeway to Funen, just outside Svendborg.

Orø In the Isefjord and almost surrounded by Zealand. Ferry from Holbæk (30 minutes) or Hammer Bakke (six minutes). 650 inhabitants. Inn, over 1,000 summerhouses. 13th century church, small museum. Scenery unexceptional.

Sejerø Thin slip of an island off the north-west coast of Zealand. Camping site. Ferry from Havnsø (60 minutes).

Agersø and Omø Two adjoining islands at the southern end of the Great Belt. Ferry from Stigsnæs, near Skælskør, on Zealand (Agersø 15 minutes, Omø 40 minutes).

Fejø and Femø A pair of islands off the north coast of Lolland. Ferry from Kragenæs (Fejø 15 minutes, Femø 50 minutes). Camping site and inn on each island.

Bogø Between Falster and Møn. Causeway from Møn linked by bridge on Farø. Ferry to Stubbekøbing, Falster (12 minutes).

HELPFUL GENERAL INFORMATION

Alphabet Don't forget that Danish has 29 letters in its alphabet. After A to Z comes Æ, Ø and Å. Bear in mind when looking in the telephone directory or any index. (The index in this guide follows the Danish style, just to get you used to it).

Banks Normal hours 9.30 a.m. to 4.00 p.m. (Thursdays 6.00 p.m.). Closed Saturdays, Sundays and public holidays.

British Embassy 40 Kastelvej, DK-2100 Copenhagen Ø. Telephone: 35 26 46 00.

Chemist In Danish it is an Apotek. It is the only place that medicine can be bought. Many preparations sold without prescription in the UK are only available on a doctor's prescription in Denmark.

Climate Danish weather, like the British variety, is variable. Summer is generally from the end of May to the end of August. It can be enjoyably warm and dry and when it is hot it is seldom humid. As you are never far from the coast there is usually a cooling breeze. Spring and autumn can be very pleasant. Bornholm has the reputation of having the best climate in Denmark.

Currency The unit of currency is the krone (plural Kroner). There are 100 øre in a krone. Coins in circulation are: 25 øre, 50 øre and 1 kr, 2 kr, 5 kr, 10 kr and 20 kr. Notes in circulation: 50 kr, 100 kr, 500 kr and 1,000 kr.

Electric current Throughout Denmark it is 220 v AC, 50 cycles. Danish plugs are not the same as those used in Britain so you will need an adaptor.

Emergencies Dial 112 from any public telephone (no charge).

Health service All employees and pensioners from EC countries and their families staying temporarily in Denmark are covered by Insurance Group 1, which entitles them to free medical care and the refund of a considerable amount of dentists' and pharmacy charges. British citizens who do not fall into the categories above are covered by Insurance Group 2 which entitles them to a more limited refund. Your UK passport or the EC form E-111D issued by your local authority has to be shown to the doctor or pharmacy. If cash payment is demanded, the refund is paid by the nearest municipal or health insurance office (details from the local tourist office). The refund should be applied for before leaving Denmark.

Although the Danish health service does cover you to a major extent, travel insurance cover is also recommended.

Passports UK visitors to Denmark need to have a standard British passport or a British visitor's passport. A visa is not required.

Post office Normal opening hours 9.00 a.m. or 10.00 a.m. to 5.00 p.m. or 5.30 p.m. Saturday 9.00 a.m. – 12 noon (some offices closed on Saturdays). Closed on Sundays.

Public holidays Maundy Thursday (day before Good Friday), Good Friday, Easter Sunday, Easter Monday; Great Prayer Day (fourth Friday after Good Friday), Ascension Day, Whit Sunday,

GENERAL INFORMATION

Whit Monday, Constitution Day (5 June, from noon); Christmas Eve (from noon), Christmas Day, Boxing Day, New Year's Eve (from noon), New Year's Day.

Radio news in English Radio Denmark broadcasts a short news bulletin in English, Monday – Saturday, at 8.15 am. on programme III (93.85 MHz).

Telephone Lift receiver and insert Dkr 1 coin (local calls) or DKr 5 or 10 (long distance calls). Important: your coins are not returned even if the number is engaged, so insert the minimum number of coins. You can repeat your call or make another one if you still have a 'credit'. For assistance in using the telephone dial 113. For international calls dial 009 followed by the country code (44 for the UK), then the STD code and finally the subscriber's number.

Tipping Almost non-existent. Hotel, restaurant and taxi charges include service and you only tip if some special service has been rendered. You don't tip hairdressers, theatre or cinema ushers. About the only exception is leaving 1 or 2 kr for use of the wash-basin in staffed ladies' or gentlemen's toilets.

Useful addresses

Danish Tourist Board UK Office: P.O. Box 2LT, London W1A 2LT. Telephone: 01-734 2637.

Copenhagen Tourist Information, Bernstorffsgade 1, DK-1577, Copenhagen V. Telephone: 33 11 13 25 for enquiries when in Denmark.

Scandinavian Seaways, Parkeston Quay, Harwich, Essex CO12 4QG. Telephone: (0255) 241234.

DFDS Travel Centre, 15 Hanover Street, London W1R 9HG.

Scandinavian Seaways, Tyne Commission Quay, North Shields, Tyne and Wear NE29 6EE. Telephone: (091) 293 6262.

VAT Called MOMS in Denmark. Current rate is 25 per cent. Normally all prices are quoted inclusive of VAT.

What you can take in Coming from the UK (as an EC country) you can take into Denmark (by persons over 17 years of age): 1.5 litres of spirits (or 3 litres of strong or sparkling wine). 3 litres of other wine (table wine). 300 cigarettes or 150 cigarillos or 75 cigars or 400 g of smoking tobacco.

As the price of spirits and cigarettes is high in Denmark it is advisable to buy your requirements on the ferry to Denmark.

INDEX

143

INDEX